Called to Remember

"*Called to Remember* is an invitation to act on the wisdom found in Deuteronomy 4:9, 'Do not forget the things your eyes have seen or let them fade from your heart.' Through the sharing of her own journey, Denise introduces the reader to remembering as a spiritual discipline. This is a timely, practical, and helpful book for every season of life, but especially for overcoming challenges."

—Michelle R. Loyd-Paige, CEO, PreachSista!

"What do you do when you are stuck? What do you do when you do not know how or if you can move forward? In *Called to Remember*, we are taken on an intimate journey of faith where we are challenged and guided to remember in order to move forward. Each chapter is a vignette of God at work. Each chapter guides the reader with key insights and the opportunity to engage in being formed by critical moments that are modeled for us by the author. Rev. Denise Posie has been a bridge person through her life and ministry. God has called her, uses her, and continues to equip her as his daughter. We can learn from the life of others who open their life to God and to each of us. Every one of us is on a journey of faith. This book takes what may be initially seen as an 'ordinary' life and shows how it is an extraordinary journey when you see how God travels with, shapes, and leads a person—day by day!"

—Jul Medenblik, President, Calvin Theological Seminary

"So how might an author begin a book with the narrative of her own joys and sorrows, growing up in a pastor's family in Detroit's Black America? And then move from narrative to testimony? And then from testimony to teaching? And then from teaching to training? Well, in Denise Posie's book, *Called to Remember*, the author does just that! She follows the whispering voice of God's Spirit as she moves from vocation to vocation and finally towards ordination in ministry. Between the lines of her book there is a celebration of joy as she finds her own voice in the challenges of ministry. And she invites us to travel along with her and to see our own vocational challenges with greater clarity."

—Ron Nydam, Professor of Pastoral Care-Emeritus, Calvin Theological Seminary

"Denise Posie's honest and vulnerable memoir is an invitation for all of us to remember what the Lord has done and to celebrate his goodness and faithfulness in our lives. Her inspirational story brings the message of the gospel to life in a way that is deeply compelling and relatable to readers. Posie's twelve stones of remembrance provide a strong framework to guide anyone through this new spiritual discipline of remembering. The reflection questions at the end of each chapter encourage deeper engagement with the content and prompt critical thinking, making the material applicable to the reader's faith formation and resulting in spiritual growth and maturity."

—Amanda Roozeboom, SERVE Director, ThereforeGo Ministries

"This is a special book which generously expands our understanding about what counts as spiritual formation. Written as a spiritual memoir, *Called to Remember* recounts God's kindness to Denise as she purposefully looks back at how her faith grew and deepened throughout her life. The act of remembering, modeled so compellingly by the author, becomes a fruitful way to grow more deeply in Christ."

—David W. Swanson, author of *Rediscipling the White Church*

"In *Called to Remember*, Rev. Denise Posie has produced a memoir that is in full keeping with God's teaching for us in Romans 8:28—'in all things God works for the good of those who love him, who have been called according to his purpose.' In looking back on the journey that God led her through, Reverend Posie demonstrates her deep faith and keen insights to recognize spiritual encounters and discover new revelations of God's grace. Throughout the work, we are challenged to recognize God's presence even in the midst of deep personal tragedy, racial animosity, and more—and to recognize how God is able to use everything to enhance our spiritual growth. This book is a must read—but more than that, engagement with it creates a discipleship journey for the reader that is definitely God ordained."

—Colin P. Watson Sr., Executive Director Emeritus, Christian Reformed Church in North America

Called to Remember

Formed by Life's Critical Moments

A SPIRITUAL MEMOIR

Denise L. Posie

RESOURCE *Publications* • Eugene, Oregon

CALLED TO REMEMBER
Formed by Life's Critical Moments

Copyright © 2025 Denise L. Posie. All rights reserved. Except for brief quotations in critical publications or reviews, no part of this book may be reproduced in any manner without prior written permission from the publisher. Write: Permissions, Wipf and Stock Publishers, 199 W. 8th Ave., Suite 3, Eugene, OR 97401.

Resource Publications
An Imprint of Wipf and Stock Publishers
199 W. 8th Ave., Suite 3
Eugene, OR 97401

www.wipfandstock.com

PAPERBACK ISBN: 979-8-3852-5433-0
HARDCOVER ISBN: 979-8-3852-5434-7
EBOOK ISBN: 979-8-3852-5435-4

Unless otherwise indicated, all Scripture quotations taken from The Holy Bible, New International Version®, NIV®. Copyright © 1973, 1978, 1984, 2011 by Biblica, Inc. Used with permission of Zondervan. All rights reserved worldwide. www.zondervan.com.

Scripture quotations marked (KJV) are taken from The Authorized (King James) Version. Rights in the Authorized Version in the United Kingdom are vested in the Crown. Reproduced by permission of the Crown's patentee, Cambridge University Press.

Scripture quotations marked (NLT) are taken from the Holy Bible, New Living Translation, copyright ©1996, 2004, 2015 by Tyndale House Foundation. Used by permission of Tyndale House Publishers, Carol Stream, Illinois 60188. All rights reserved.

Contents

Acknowledgments ix

Introduction xi

1 Dreams for a Better Life 1

2 Early Memories of Love, Resilience, and Forgiveness 9

3 Oh, Happy Day! 17

4 Seven Years Were Enough 26

5 Launching into the Unknown 36

6 Waiting for the Peach Cobbler 46

7 Oh, Taste and See! 60

8 Grace on the Obstacle Course 73

9 The Unfolding of an Undeniable Conviction 81

10 Now, That's Love 94

11 A Glimpse of a Heavenly Vision 105

12 Was It Worth It? 113

APPENDIX 1 We Will Not Forget! A Prayer 123

APPENDIX 2 Stones of Remembrance at a Glance 125

APPENDIX 3 A Model for Remembering God's Goodness 130

APPENDIX 4 The Stages in the Life of Faith: *The Critical Journey* 132

Bibliography 135

Acknowledgments

I HAD NO IDEA what I was getting myself into when I began writing *Called to Remember*. I owe everything I've accomplished thus far to God, the Father, Jesus, the Son, and the Holy Spirit's guidance, which led me to start a spiritual journal shortly after becoming a Christian, without knowing that one day I would write a book. I never became disinterested in the theme of remembering what God has done. It stayed on my mind and in my heart.

I'm reminded of my angel on the Delta flight 1619, who told me, "He [God] will impart what you need by placing you in the path of people who have what you need. He's going to bless you for what you've done." These words ring true to me today, just as they did many years ago. I sensed the Spirit placing me on a path of connecting with people who had what I needed, and I was willing to ask because, ultimately, I knew God would provide.

It was clear to me from the beginning that I needed someone like author Anna Redsand to help me with navigating the writing process. We didn't know each other prior, but God gave me someone who could bring out the best me. She probed for clarity, gave me feedback, affirmed my writing style, and edited my early manuscript. I'm deeply indebted to the gift of her companionship on this journey.

Thank you to Heather Carraher, Savanah Landerholm, Hannah Starr, and the Resource Publications team for their attentiveness and wonderful support in the completion of this project.

While studying in the DMin in leadership and spiritual formation program at Portland Seminary, I benefited from the expertise of my project advisors and faculty, including Jeney Park-Hearn, MaryKay Morse, and Ken Van Vliet. Their contributions led me to areas of research that I would never have discovered on my own. The weekly virtual engagements and in-person spiritual retreat at the Cannon Beach Conference Center with

Acknowledgments

my cohort, the Weavers, were the highlights of my experience and personal growth.

I'm forever grateful to Javonna Allen, Ken Baker, Dave Beelen, Dorothy Jenkins, David Malone, and Amanda Roozeboom for their willingness to participate in a discovery workshop. They shared personal experiences and wisdom regarding the challenges pastors and leaders face in paying attention to their spiritual encounters as part of spiritual and faith formation. My individual virtual conversations as part of the discovery process with Danjuma Gibson, Nancy James, and Ron Nydam stretched my imagination and sharpened my focus. Their lifelong professional expertise in their respective areas was invaluable.

I appreciate Jerome and Kelly Daley, Callie Feyen, Scott Hoezee, Erin Richer, Mark and Patricia Scheffers, Freida Watson, and Idella Posey-Whitfield for their willingness to give feedback on chapter drafts from various perspectives, including those of teacher, preacher, pastor, spiritual director, writer, and ministry leader. I am grateful to the expertise offered by Michelle Loyd-Paige, Jul Medenblik, Ron Nydam, Bob Price, Amanda Roozeboom, David Swanson, and Colin Watson in providing helpful feedback on individual chapters or the entire manuscript. I value the encouragement and cheers from the sidelines throughout the entire writing process: my sisters Deborah and Donna, cousin Cheryl, and close friends Jan Baker, Jackie Cantrell, Yvonne Frederick, Norma Daniel-Jones, and Gwen Vassar. I thank them and a host of others, including Calvin Theological Seminary staff and faculty, who asked from time to time, "How's the book coming?" Several people prayed for me, and I appreciate their prayers. The Spirit kept me going, and not once did I think about quitting. I'm forever grateful.

Introduction

Lord, all that I have discovered about you I have done so by remembering.
—Augustine

One time in our Circle of Remembering, we had been discussing how past spiritual encounters affect the present. One mature pastor had just told a story from his childhood. "It was after church," he said, "and for some reason, I was the last person to come to the door and shake the minister's hand, feeling very grown-up." We giggled.

"I was about to leave that grown-up feeling behind and run out to chase the other boys on the grass in front of the church, but the pastor put his hand on my shoulder and said, 'Wait a minute, Pete, there's something I've been meaning to say to you, and this is a good time.' I looked around and realized there was no one there but the pastor and me. He said, 'I've been watching you grow in your love for the Lord and his word. I see how often you share that love by asking intriguing questions in our after-school group and showing other boys and girls ways to follow Jesus. I think that God has placed a call on your life to be a pastor.' I heard the sincerity in his voice. I don't remember saying anything, and I'm pretty sure I ran right out afterward to play with my friends. Funny, I never thought about that until now." Pete was quiet then, looking thoughtful.

When I got home that evening, I reflected on Pete's story. I imagined the power his pastor's words may have had during Pete's boyhood and, maybe, to a greater extent, without his awareness, as he discerned his call to ministry. Maybe while in seminary or when he felt the laying on of hands at his ordination. However, I don't know if he would remember this spiritual encounter if he got into a challenging pastoral role and doubted his call.

Introduction

What if we forget our spiritual encounters as a part of spiritual formation? That would be regretful, especially if we find ourselves in transition, at a crossroads, or uncertain. A spiritual encounter gets our attention. It is not merely a memory of something that happened in the past; it's a demonstration of God's goodness shown to us. It's life-giving and supernatural! *Called to Remember* shows my incredible journey of remembering through sometimes painful situations. I offer my spiritual memoir as a guide to encourage us to stay focused, hopeful, and anchored in the Lord as the Spirit leads us through life situations and spiritual formation. I use one of twelve stones of remembrance at the end of each chapter to show how God got my attention and the Spirit led me through a situation to strengthen, shape, and reveal himself to me in unimaginable ways. Thomas Rausch says, "These are moments of grace in our lives, moments that can sustain us in more difficult times."[1] They quiet the voices in my head because they represent how God has revealed himself to me.

Life is filled with spiritual encounters that inform, transform, and shape our lives. These encounters might also be called "God moments," "God sightings," "promptings," "divine appointments or interventions," "the presence of God," or "holy moments." Often, they have no specific name. However, there is a sense that God has claimed a person's attention through the Holy Spirit, Scripture, an individual like Pete's pastor, or a life circumstance. Holy encounters are given for specific reasons, not always recognized at the time, and they are part of spiritual formation.

God moments require our attention and a willingness to listen deeply and obey, although the listening and the subsequent action may take place later, leading to the fulfillment of God's intention. We are called to remember these God sightings, not forget them, and apply them to our present and future. *Called to Remember* invites readers to remember our incredible, sacred, and transformational God stories.

Ironically, it is often when the reminder of a past spiritual encounter is most needed that we forget. When we are in trouble, when our backs are against the wall, we can be so overwhelmed by the pain and fear of the moment, the feeling that there is no way out or forward, that we forget God's goodness, the difficulties and the high points God has already led us through. But forgetting our past spiritual encounters hinders us in discerning God's plans for our present and future. When we forget God and what he has done for us, it may seem like what he did for us was insignificant.

---

1. Rausch, *Ignatian Retreat*, 18.

Introduction

When we forget, we don't anticipate what he might do in our present situation. We fail to tell others about his goodness. Forgetting what God has done for us may even cause us to forget God himself, though not intentionally or permanently.

I was privileged to serve as a congregational consultant in my denomination for three years. I joined a team with a long history of coming alongside individuals in ministry transition. Consultations could last for two visits, several months, or more than a year. The meetings varied in intensity, length, and outcome. Pastors, ministry leaders, and congregations sought answers about what should come next; often, there was a question of whether to stay together or separate.

On one such occasion, I sat in a church conference room with one of my team colleagues and the church's pastor. I listened to the pastor explain his understanding of the conflict between him and the church leadership and what he felt he needed to consider before deciding whether to stay or leave.

I wondered if there had been anything from the pastor's past that might help him understand how to respond in the present. Had God revealed anything to him that would be helpful now? What if he were to engage in the spiritual practice of remembering a God encounter—a practice that could replenish his soul as he navigated this church conflict? Was he so immersed in the present situation that he couldn't reach back to cling to a word, a statement, or a Scripture verse from his past that might inform him about what to do? Would such a practice have been helpful?

Over time, questions like these grew and became a burden on my heart for pastors, ministry leaders, and congregations, especially when the pastor had left after a conflict, whether voluntarily or involuntarily. I wondered what "burning bush" experience they might have received from the Spirit, their parents, a Sunday school teacher, a pastor, or someone else—an encounter that might have caused them to pay attention. Had they possibly forgotten what God had done for them in past circumstances, so they were now experiencing anxiety, depression, fear, or insecurity? Did they not know that God is good, even in difficult times? Would a practice of remembering have brought about a different outcome?

I was concerned about how quickly we forget what God has done for us when a crisis comes, and we find ourselves at a crossroads. We sometimes look for the easiest or preferred way forward when life becomes uncomfortable. Sometimes, we forget or ignore the power of God's goodness

Introduction

in the past and how the memory of that can guide us through the present. By contrast, we are reminded in Deut 4:9, "Do not forget the things your eyes have seen or let them fade from your heart as long as you live."

Questions from my pastoral and consultation work persisted. In 2022, when I studied in the doctor of ministry in leadership and spiritual formation program at Portland Seminary in Oregon, I chose to focus on what others were saying about the spiritual practice of remembering. Within my seminary cohort and my community of believers, I investigated how remembering our spiritual encounters relates to spiritual formation. I researched biblical, theological, historical, psychological, and cultural evidence for how remembering nourishes us, refreshes us, and supports us in times of difficulty and discernment.

Historically and culturally, for instance, as an African American, I identify the end of slavery in America with the Israelites' deliverance from Egyptian bondage and also the Year of Jubilee, freeing slaves as described in the book of Leviticus. This African American collective memory forms a spiritual encounter that transcends centuries and generations. Recalling what God did for us and this country liberates my soul and propels me to press on. My strength comes from remembering God's goodness to me, to a people, and a country. The research confirmed what I've seen of liberation from other cultural and ethnic atrocities worldwide, often recognized by holidays, reunions, memorials, and other rituals of remembrance. Those memories are meant to renew faith and trust.

My research helped me expand my vision of a spiritual practice of remembering as part of spiritual formation. Through my reading of *The Critical Journey: Stages in the Life of Faith* by Janet Hagberg and Robert Guelich, I discovered a connection between spiritual formation and remembering our spiritual encounters. At the end of my first year of doctoral studies, it was time to write, using what I'd learned. I didn't know all the details, but I felt compelled to share what God had taught me about himself, myself, and others by telling my own stories of God moments and how the practice of remembering them sustained me in critical times. I couldn't share everything, so I've included in my book what was most crucial from my more than thirty years of journaling about my God encounters, sometimes through painful transitions.

The essence of *Called to Remember* is spiritual formation and transformation, love and surrender, perseverance and forgiveness, healing and restoration. I show how these practices and gifts affect our calling and how

Introduction

we may live into it. Early on, I realized that God was cultivating a loving relationship with me; thus, I began the story with some of my early memories, embracing my whole self and showing the uniqueness and dynamics of my family, neighborhood, and community.

These stories can be a source of power in understanding our past, present, and future—the power to shut out opposing forces coming against us and to open our hearts to how God chooses to use them for his glory. I see light and darkness in my life, and God uses it all. God has called me, as he calls all of us, to remember what he has done for us, deepening our love and trust as his witnesses in a broken world.

Called to Remember is not simply the story of my God moments. I hope to engage the reader in exploring how our times of transition, uncertainties, and the unknown can intersect with what God has done in the past, leading us to a fuller understanding of the present and future. Our memories have implications beyond the events' initial occurrence; they have the potential to be life-giving encounters with the power to inform and transform.

To the pastor, ministry leader, minister in training, or layperson, *Called to Remember: Formed by Life's Critical Moments* is offered as a guide to help the reader stay focused, hopeful, and anchored in the Lord as the Spirit leads us through life situations. The book shows how remembering spiritual encounters can provide answers that help us remain faithful to our calling and, sometimes, to know whether to stay in or leave a situation. I hope the reader will discover the relationship between past and present spiritual encounters as a pathway to replenishing the soul, renewing confidence and strength for following God's will. The intention is that the book will lead you to regularly practice remembering your spiritual encounters as God's plan for your growth. These are redemptive, restorative, and transformative moments and are not meant to be forgotten but to be life-giving.

You might be stretched by my spiritual encounters and how I experience the Spirit's activities in my life. That is all right, but it is important for you to remain open to receive whatever the Spirit desires to teach you.

May you pause and pray as you reflect on your spiritual journey while reading about mine. This might be a good time to start a spiritual practice of journaling or finding another way to remember by recording what is revealed. This can be a time to consider what the Holy Spirit is saying to us in our situations. Where in our life are we experiencing anxiety and unrest? Where are we finding calm and rest? What are we being called to remember

Introduction

from our past to speak to our present and future? God uses individuals and the body of Christ to shape and lead us. Who has he placed in our path? For what reason(s)?

What I offer the reader is not a prescription or remedy for remembering what God has done, but it is a testament to the life-giving reality of the Holy Spirit's work, leading me in unforeseen and unimaginable ways to live my best new life in Christ.

Called to Remember attempts to ignite a fire in us to pay attention, listen, meditate, discern, and respond to our God encounters. At the end of each chapter, I have connected my holy moment with a stone of remembrance and invite you to use the reflection questions to respond and connect your holy moment with your stone of remembrance.

After the Israelites had finished crossing the Jordan River into the promised land in Josh 4, the Lord told Joshua to choose twelve men to find twelve stones in the middle of the Jordan in front of where the priest had stood carrying the ark of the covenant. Each man should carry a stone, representing the twelve tribes, to where they were staying. These stones were a memorial for God cutting off the flow of the Jordan, where the priests stood until all the Israelites had crossed. They arrived at Gilgal, where they were staying, and set up the stones. It was their responsibility to obey God when their children asked about the stones—they would talk about what God had done for them in crossing the Jordan and remind them that God did the same for the previous generation in parting the Red Sea.

While talking to a colleague one day, he used the phrase "generational faithfulness," symbolizing a trail of God's goodness from one generation to the next generation. Our divine moments are a powerful testimony of God's presence and goodness to us, and we're responsible for telling our stories.

Further guidance for the practice of remembering is offered in the appendices. One of my most valuable insights is this: remembering is not about us but about God—who he is and what he does for us. If we have the capacity to remember what God has done in our lives, but we forget to do that, we can be tempted to take credit for what he deserves—all the glory. May we embrace *Called to Remember*—in the name of God the Father, the Son, and the Holy Spirit. Amen.

1

Dreams for a Better Life

A significant truth of the gospel is that our stories are uniquely given to us, in order to help others recognize the value and uniqueness of their own stories.
—Keith Anderson

In the 1940s, my parents packed their clothes and got into the car with my dad's older brother to move from Alabama to Detroit, with no intent to go back. Over six million blacks moved from rural life in the South to urban life in the North from 1916–1970, known as the Great Migration.[1]

Although my father was concerned about leaving his mother behind, his oldest brother and sister lived nearby. My mother said goodbye and hugged her mother, brother, and three sisters as they stood on a few acres of land that had belonged to their family for many years.

My paternal grandfather was an African Methodist Episcopal Church pastor, and my maternal grandfather had been a laborer in the building of the Wilson Dam on the Tennessee River in Alabama. Both grandfathers had died before my parents' move.

Mom held my parents' only child and son in her arms as she sat in the backseat for the twelve-hour drive to Detroit, where many came to work in the factories of the Big Three: Chrysler, Ford, and General Motors corporations. Everyone who took this path had dreams for a better life.

Shortly after they arrived, my parents moved to a large, two-story boarding house where other young couples and their children lived. It was

---

1. National Archives, "Great Migration."

a suitable accommodation for the stay-at-home moms and working dads. The boarding house was more than living quarters. The owners, the Macdonalds, an older Christian couple, nurtured these young couples as if they were their children. Without their nurture and care, life would have been more difficult. They encouraged young couples to save money to purchase their own homes by providing affordable single rooms and community spaces. They extended grace and love that was not forgotten.

A boarding house was a common living situation for migrants newly arrived from the South. My parents were fortunate to find this accommodation in the North End district through my dad's siblings, who had moved to Detroit a couple of years earlier. Many migrants from the South, like my parents, moved to the North End or to the Black Bottom. They knew where and where not to go, already aware of the city's housing discrimination.

Before blacks moved in, the North End was predominately Jewish. By 1940, it was 40 percent black, and a major takeover occurred in the 1950s with a robust population of blacks moving in, opening small stores, repurposing a Jewish synagogue as a church, and establishing places for nightlife.[2]

When their second son was born, limited space made it difficult to continue living in the boarding house. My parents bought a white-wood frame, four-bedroom, two-story home with a one-and-a-half bathroom and a large fenced-in backyard on the northwest side in the late forties. Three baby girls were born about two years apart in the early to late fifties. My mom's best friend was our next-door neighbor. We were heartbroken when Betty, her husband, and their five-year-old son moved further north to the suburbs when I was eight. Theirs was probably among the last white families to move out of a soon-to-be predominately black neighborhood. As I recall, we, the children, didn't understand why they moved. Our parents never commented on why. Most children my age during the years we called "white flight" had a little white friend and family move to the suburbs. Nevertheless, we did keep in touch with each other during sicknesses, deaths, and the birth of grandchildren, and even after our parents had passed away. Friendships were meaningful to our family and neighborhood.

I was born in Detroit in 1954, the year the US Supreme Court made a critical decision in the Brown v. Board of Education case, determining that segregated public schools were unconstitutional. The US Supreme Court upheld the Brown v. Board of Education decision to integrate public

---

2. Elliott et al., *North End*, 32–33.

schools, bringing America into a critical time of transition. Before this decision, schools in the United States were allowed to discriminate based on an individual's race under the Plessy v. Ferguson decision, which allowed separate but presumably equal public accommodations.[3]

Six years after the Brown v. Board of Education decision, little Ruby Bridges, the same age as I was, walked bravely through the doors of the all-white William Frantz Elementary School in New Orleans, escorted by US Marshals. "White parents in Louisiana vehemently protested the idea, and school boards and politicians sought to block desegregation in the state."[4]

I was unaware of racial discrimination at Hally Elementary School, where my siblings and I went. A few black teachers and several white teachers and administrators worked in a predominately black, socioeconomically diverse community. Our parents were a mixture of business owners, doctors, educators, and factory and government workers. I felt cared for and was an active, happy, and capable elementary school student, enjoying choir, gym, music, Future Teachers' Club, after-school ballet, and good friends.

My father drove the Detroit Street Railway (DSR) city buses until he retired after a long career. Once, I waited on the corner of our street for my dad to meet me during his last bus route for the day before returning to the bus terminal. I jumped on the bus and proudly sat behind him on a long bench-like seat to see and hear the change drop in the bus fare box. I enjoyed how my dad interacted with the people and their respectful responses. He rarely missed a day at work. He had many unused, paid sick days that enabled him to retire a year early.

On Saturdays, sometimes I drove our second car back and forth in our wire-fenced backyard. Of course, my dad sat in the front seat with me, ready to take the steering wheel if necessary. Fortunately, it was never necessary. Dad was known for always tinkering with his second car. The family's primary car was off limits for my driving lessons.

Although my father did not go to high school, he liked to learn. He wrote comments in the margins of his books. He took a course to become a locksmith, where he received and completed the assignments through mail-in. He even taught my sister Donna his side trade.

One of my fondest memories was seeing my father kneeling beside my parents' bed, praying with his head in his hands as I passed by their

3. National Archives, "Brown v. Board."
4. Dawson, "Ruby Bridges," para. 4.

bedroom. I felt he knew God was with him, which is how he communed with him. He read his Bible often. I recall pulling up a chair at the dining room table when he had opened his Bible to the Gospel of John. He welcomed my company and attention as I listened and followed his finger as he read.

Once, my dad and I attended an evening service at New Bethel Baptist Church to hear the late Rev. C. L. Franklin preach—the father of the Queen of Soul, Aretha Franklin. We were blessed with seats in the balcony along with hundreds of other people. The choir's singing raised the roof, and people danced down the aisles in the joy of the Lord. I had never witnessed such joy in the churches I had attended. Reverend Franklin was a powerful, eloquent preacher. The people shouted, "Amen," "Tell the truth, Pastor," and "Preach, Doc!" The call and response was rhythmic. It was a treat to be in the auditorium instead of listening to the service on the radio.

My mother worked nights as a nurse's aide in two nursing homes for most of our school years. She liked telling stories about Dad and her working together in the field, picking cotton when they were young. She claimed to pick cotton faster than him. He would smile every time she said that. When I see a cotton field in their hometown in Alabama, I always think about the little money and great sacrifices they made while laboring in the hot sun under poor working conditions. Sometimes, I smile to keep from crying and deeply thinking about that time in history.

The time spent with our mom was eventful. It was a treat to regularly go with her to the local resale store. When we walked into the store, Esther, the owner, a middle-aged Jewish woman, would wave her hand and say, "Hello, Mrs. Posie."

Mom responded, "How are you doing?" Esther was energized whenever regular customers came to her store. Mom was a wise shopper, and she did not waste time.

On special occasions like Easter Sunday, we went to the New Center area to one of the finest department stores in Detroit for our new dresses. From a distance, you could see the large letters, "Demery's," as we approached the business district that included the famous General Motors and Fisher buildings. Mom dressed well, especially on Sundays. She kept her three girls looking nice. Even today, I like to look nice and wear clothes with color against my brown skin and styles compatible with my personality.

My mother grew up in a Missionary Baptist church. Her extended family still belongs to the church she attended as a child. I visit Mt. Olive Missionary Baptist Church every time I go to Alabama. I am family.

My mother was a woman of faith. She believed all things were possible for God and read the Bible. Psalm 23 was her favorite. She also listened to preachers on the radio, like evangelist Oral Roberts. She was often asked to recite a well-known African American Christian poem in church programs. She frequently sang while she washed dishes. I could hear her in the kitchen singing, "I Want Jesus to Walk with Me," "I Will Trust in the Lord," or "On the Battlefield." These were her favorites, and we enjoyed hearing her sing. I find myself singing those same songs every now and then.

My parents became members of a small church at the end of our street, Northwest Unity Baptist Church, where Gregory, Deborah, Donna, and I were baptized. Northwest Unity is where my father and a few other young men attended training from the pastor in preparation to become ordained ministers.

Women served as soloists, ushers, and deaconesses who prepared the Lord's Supper, and there was a unique group of highly respected, seasoned women called the Mothers' Board. They were often sought for counsel and wisdom concerning church matters. I do not recall women reading Scripture aloud in church unless it was in Sunday school. The pastor, Rev. Ozzie Clark, was like a friend to our family. He sometimes came to the house on his way to the church.

As I recall, my understanding of the Holy Spirit was when someone got "happy" during a song or the pastor's sermon. I saw, heard, and experienced the person's joy because they were grateful for what God had done in their life. It got my attention, but I didn't quite understand.

When I was in high school, my father founded a small Baptist church about four miles from home. There were a few faithful members, including my family. I did not attend regularly because I had become a member of a Baptist church within walking distance of my parents' house. I became a member because it was a bigger church; the ushers standing at the door were welcoming. Young people were actively involved in church life. People were drawn to its uplifting singing—anthems, gospels, and Negro spirituals. We had contemporary Christian plays written by our choir director and performed on stage in the auditorium at Detroit's Wayne State University. We traveled out of state one summer and visited other churches in the Detroit area frequently.

In our home, one parent was always at home with the children until we finished junior high school. They made sure we were never left unattended as children at night. As teenagers, we often visited our oldest brother, Frank, who had cognitive and minor physical limitations. He lived in Battle Creek, Michigan, at the Fort Custer State Home until he was a young adult, when our parents brought him home permanently. A few times one of our brother's white friends, Dennis, who did not have family nearby, came to our house to stay overnight.

Weekends were fun. Our family visited Palmer Park and Belle Isle Park regularly. We put on our ice skates in the winter and headed to the frozen pond at Palmer Park. In the summer, we played on the swings and teeter-totter. While sitting on the banks of a small pond at Belle Isle Park, I had my eyes set on where I wanted to cast my bamboo fishing pole when I accidentally hooked the back of Dad's head. He ordered me to "Go down farther." Everyone laughed. I moved quickly.

The beauty of the community was found in our local neighborhood through the interactions between neighborhood children in our front and backyards. We named ourselves the Alden Street Kids. It was not unusual for children to play in front of our house. Girls sat on the porch playing jacks or just having fun. Or they jumped rope and played hopscotch in front of the house. Boys and girls ran the bases in softball and built and raced go-karts in the alley. One winter, Gregory made an ice rink in the backyard for neighborhood children to skate on. That took skill, time, not stepping onto the ice too soon, and a lot of water. Gregory also loved animals and drawing pictures of them. When neighborhood kids could not come over, the four Posie kids made their own fun, like playing with pet turtles or rabbits in the backyard.

Looking back at my early experiences, I see how fortunate we were to have had good, loving, and caring parents, extended families in Detroit and Alabama, neighbors who knew our names and parents, and church communities. Our neighborhood was made up of singles (men and women), singles with children, and married families with and without children. Everything was not perfect, but everything was good. We had enough. Our neighbors supported each other during difficult times.

We did not usually say "I love you" to each other in my family, but we knew we were loved because of how we cared for each other. My parents worked hard to provide for us, which is an expression of love. Today, though, I wish we had designated times for daily gatherings as a family at the dining room table to hear and study God's word and pray together. We needed more than a prayer before a meal; however, seeds were planted. We were taught to pray every night. I remember putting my hands together repeating,

> Now I lay me down to sleep; I pray the Lord my soul to keep.
> If I die before I wake, I pray the Lord my soul to take.

I wish we had set aside time to share our personal experiences and receive wise advice. We had heard about some of our parents' blessings and struggles, but now I wish I had heard more, especially about how they faced racism. It would have helped me understand my roots better. Today, I acknowledge my "unique story," and I fully embrace who I am.

Looking back, I see that my mother was strong-willed and kind, but opinionated, and she did not always seek to understand me; nor did I seek to understand her. I knew I loved my mother, and she loved me.

Growing up, I thought my father was weak. The Lord later showed me that my father was strong, although he was quiet. I had thought strength equated to having the most prominent voice and presence, and weakness was being quiet and unseen. This was my assumption.

My parents had been married for fifty-two years before our father passed. My mother died seven years later. I will never forget the words of a clergy colleague and friend, Rev. Al Mulder, who left a message on my voicemail after he learned of my father's passing.

"Denise, I am sorry to hear about your father's death. May the Lord teach you 'more' about who he was, now since he is gone." I gasped, but that is precisely what God did. I felt good about who my father was. I knew I loved him, and he loved me.

STONE OF REMEMBRANCE: HOPE

God had brought my parents and ancestors through troubling times in America during Jim Crow and slavery. I am shaped by their hope for tomorrow. I will remember seeing my father praying and my mother singing as she washed the dishes. According to Rom 12:12, we are to "be joyful in hope, patient in affliction, faithful in prayer." God gives us hope.

REFLECTION QUESTIONS

What images do you have of your parents or the people who raised you that have influenced your knowledge and relationship with God or spiritual practices? When do you recall these images? What impact do they have on you? What is your stone of remembrance?

2

Early Memories of Love, Resilience, and Forgiveness

> There is a healing way to remember the wrongs of our irreversible past, a way that can bring hope for the future along with our sorrow for the past. Redemptive remembering keeps a clear picture of the past, but it adds a new setting and shifts its focus. —Lewis B. Smedes

THE JANGLING OF THE phone woke me from a sound sleep. I looked at my alarm clock and saw it was after midnight. I heard Mom get up, still half asleep. She called out, "I got it." Then, "Come on, James, we have to go." She rushed upstairs to our rooms. "That was the police," she said, her voice trembling and eyes filled with tears. "It's Gregory. He's been shot. We're going to the hospital."

I was fourteen.

I couldn't get back to sleep, my imagination running. I thought about Gregory. I'd wondered for a long time already if we'd one day get a call that he'd been involved in a serious situation with no easy way out. Then I imagined my parents as they made the twenty-minute drive to the hospital. Did their silence fill the car? Did fearful thoughts run through their minds? Blame? More importantly, did they think Gregory was going to be all right?

My two sisters, Deborah and Donna, went back to their room. I stayed in bed for a little while. Then I dressed and took the bus to school. I needed to get out of the house. The walls felt like they were closing in on me. I felt like walking and breathing fresh air. I wanted to forget this bad news ever happened. I couldn't focus on anything but Gregory's condition.

When I got on the bus, I found a window seat and held myself together. I stared out the window, looking for answers. Shortly after I went inside Mumford High School, I heard the last bell ring and saw a few stragglers behind me. I looked down the long, quiet, calming, light blue hallway, and I kept walking, my face turned toward the lockers. I slipped in and out of the girls' bathroom, the study hall, and the counselor's office. I volunteered for Dr. Stewart once a week, and he allowed me to sit in his waiting area. When lunchtime came, I decided to go back home. I felt Gregory wouldn't make it, although I prayed for him to pull through.

It turned out Gregory and two young black men, Michael and Jerome, had robbed the cigarette machine in a local bar. Someone saw them and called the police before they could leave the property. Jerome managed to get away, but Gregory and Michael ran in the opposite direction. They were shot by the first police officer to respond. Gregory had a head wound and was in critical condition. Michael was shot in the leg. I wonder now if Gregory was shot first. In those days, a black man running from the police would inevitably end in a shooting, or death. Michael survived and would later serve time in prison. When our parents got home, they told us that Gregory, their second-born, our brother, had died that morning.

His death was the most tragic thing we ever experienced as a family. We were heartbroken. We responded by doing what we always saw our parents do in times of trouble: take it to the Lord in prayer. Sometimes, when Mom was heavily burdened, she'd look up and moan, "Lord, have mercy," seeking God's strength to face the challenge. She had enough faith to believe the Lord would bring our family through a tough time. I just knew it; I'd watched her before. But this was her son.

Dad had long carried the weight of his firstborn having special needs, and now his second son was dead. He'd hoped Gregory would follow in his footsteps as a minister, even with a past that seemed incorrigible. He believed God could change Gregory's life. Neither my father nor mother excessively expressed their grief in front of us, nor do I recall overhearing any emotional outbursts from their bedroom at night when I went upstairs to my room.

Gregory's life was gone. It seemed so final. Our family sat in the first row of seats at the funeral home visitation. I saw many young people around Gregory's age stand in line to say goodbye and greet our family.

Early Memories of Love, Resilience, and Forgiveness

We were comforted and cared for there. Gregory had a likable personality, and he was intelligent and handsome. Our family and friends in Alabama poured out that same love and care at the funeral service and interment in our family cemetery. We cried and held each other closely. We were proud to be his sisters.

I learned that time does not cease; it continues with or without us. Memories last. As far as I know, my family and I moved with time instead of getting stuck. Gregory would never be with us again, but we believed he was with his Lord. We will never forget him.

During the late 1960s, many young black boys and men were killed in violent police-involved cases. Blacks and law enforcement in Detroit had a long history of poor race and community relations, even before the riots in 1967.

About ten years after Gregory's death, I worked as an administrative assistant at the Detroit Police Department's main headquarters downtown, first with the deputy chief and then in internal affairs in the late 1970s.

I was often in the office by myself. Whenever I glanced at the old, army-green file cabinet, I was tempted to find the investigative report of Gregory's death. I hesitated until one day, while I was about to file some documents, I felt the time was right. I was not concerned about being interrupted. It was not unusual for me to file reports, and I was determined to see Gregory's.

I stepped away from my desk and walked toward the file cabinet. I pulled the drawer open. My fingers flipped through many folders until I found the report of my brother's case. I wondered who had filed the report and if it had ever been looked at again. It struck me as strange that every file in the drawer was the story of a dead person involved in an altercation with the police.

I took a deep breath. I slowly opened the folder. I saw photos of the crime scene and Gregory's body in the morgue. I looked briefly at the typed name and signature of the police officer, a white man under investigation for the shooting.

No tears flowed down my face as they had on the day he died. My breathing was slow and light. I was brokenhearted that he was no longer here. I prayed and shook my head, "Lord, have mercy."

I could not have done this alone, but I was determined. Years later, I realized I had a spiritual encounter then. God was present. He did not speak to me, but I sensed his presence in the silence. No hatred, bitterness, or anger emerged from my heart. I could not have composed myself as I did on my own. My hands were steady. My mind was present. This profound moment and that space were sacred that day, unlike any other day.

I thought, "The *officer* did not have to kill Gregory." There had been no threat. None of the young men carried weapons. I prayed for *the officer* as I fixed my eyes on his first and last name. I knew many Detroit police, but not this one. I returned the folder and stayed at work until the end of my workday.

Years later, I was with my sisters, Deborah and Donna, at our parents' house for a regular drop-in visit. I told them, "I read the investigative report of Gregory's death when I worked at the police department." They looked at each other as we sat around the dining room table.

I paused, then said, "I decided not to tell Mom and Dad because it was painful for all of us." Deborah and Donna said nothing, perhaps choosing not to remember.

As I write this, I sit in front of my computer, looking outside through the small openings in the horizontal blinds. I imagine a different outcome for our family tragedy.

Gregory, Michael, and Jerome have run to the back door, when they are discovered having robbed the cigarette machine.

The responding officer shouts, "Police, police! Stop! Stop!"

They freeze with their hands raised so they can be seen. The backup scout car arrives on the scene, and two officers leave the cruiser while the first officer aims his revolver at the young men.

"Get on the ground, facedown, and do not move. I said get on the ground now."

"What do we have here?" the first new arrival asks and is briefed on the situation.

"Handcuff them."

Gregory and his friends cooperate as each is made to get in the back seat. The officers take them to the Tenth Precinct, ten minutes away from the crime scene. The next day, they are taken for arraignment to hear the charges brought against them.

The judge asks, "Do you have an attorney?"

All three respond, "No."

"Then, one will be appointed for each of you. Do you understand?"

"Yes, sir." They are scared by this time.

Early Memories of Love, Resilience, and Forgiveness

The judge sets the bond and the date for their court appearance, where they will receive the probable charges and sentences. They are returned to jail.

As I continue with my imaginary scenario, *at home, the phone rings the next day, around seven o'clock in the morning. We're about to leave the house for school, and Mom answers the phone. She can barely hear the soft trembling voice of the male caller.*

"*Who is this? What's wrong? Speak louder.*"

It's Gregory, calling to tell my parents about the trouble he's in.

"*I'm sorry, Momma. I'm in jail.*"

There is a long silence. Then she says shortly, "We'll be there."

My parents plan to see him later that morning before his court appearance. They will pay the bond for his release. He's scared because he will likely be sent to prison. This isn't his first offense, but it is his first felony.

At trial, the young men receive a prison sentence that fits the crime.

Even today, such a situation could have a worse outcome than the one I've imagined here, but some, though certainly not enough, reforms have been made in policing. It's easy to forget that history influences and shapes who we are, where and how we live, and how we are all affected by inhumane conditions in our communities and world. It has a residual effect on everyone.

We will not forget Gregory.

Today, I wish our family had sat around the dining room table together to share stories after his funeral, as a "ritual of remembrance." What was he like as a baby? Or a little boy? Why wasn't he smiling in the picture where he stands next to a white Santa Claus? Why wasn't he sitting on Santa's lap? Did he want to be there? When do you think he was happiest as a boy and as a young adult? Did he have dreams? What did he talk about?

We would recall these stories through the eyes of Gregory's parents and siblings—Frank, Deborah, Denise, and Donna—and celebrate and remember him profoundly. I've since learned that remembering is a balm to the soul. It can be part of the healing process, and memories of our loved ones are empowering to present and future generations. Remembering sustains our souls and helps us see where God was present in our loved one's life. That is the beauty and power of remembering.

Before I saw the investigative report of my brother's death, I knew I had forgiven him for what he had done and forgiven the officer for firing the fatal gunshot. My willingness to forgive was beyond my understanding as a teenager. Still, I knew it was right because my parents modeled forgiving others without being critical or angry about being wronged.

In the Broadway musical *Hamilton*, a line in the song "It's Quiet Uptown" describes forgiveness as "a grace too powerful to name."[1] Josie Schuman, managing editor of the *Carroll News* in Hillsville, Virginia, notes that it is well known that black families and the loved ones of those killed by police brutality and/or racial violence have seldom resorted to acts of resentment or vengeance.[2] The act of forgiveness is beyond human understanding under these horrific circumstances. It is a miracle. Forgiveness is the beginning of the healing process. This does not negate or minimize the loss, suffering, and pain. Grace is God's unmerited favor. It cannot be earned. When I forgave Gregory and the police officer, it did not mean they deserved my forgiveness, but it was my choice. It was for my benefit, not theirs. Forgiveness is a process, and sometimes the journey of healing takes a while. I learned not to compare myself with others because everyone grieves and handles situations differently. Grace dispensed to others is reflective of our awareness of God's grace dispensed to us. There is a mystery in the act of forgiveness.

I have heard people in the media draw the conclusion that black people forgive white people too easily and quickly in response to tragic events. Some say we are naïve and too forgiving in matters of racial disparities in policing.

In the TV movie *Finding Forrester*, William Forrester (Sean Connery), an eccentric, reclusive novelist, and Jamal Wallace (Rob Brown), a young, brilliant scholar-athlete, have a unique mentoring relationship. One of Jamal's professors, Robert Crawford (F. Murray Abraham), allowed his assumptions about blacks to inhibit his acceptance of Jamal's giftedness and scholarship as a student at a high school of excellence in Manhattan, New York. Crawford accepted Jamal's basketball gift, but he challenged his scholastic gifts.

In his mentoring role, Forrester asked Jamal,

> FORRESTER: Do you know what people are most afraid of?
> JAMAL: What?

---

1. Miranda, "It's Quiet Uptown."
2. Schuman, "Black Forgiveness."

FORRESTER: What they don't understand. And when we don't understand, we turn to our assumptions. Professor Crawford turned to his assumptions. He doesn't understand.[3]

People resort to their assumptions when they don't understand why blacks forgive in such horrific police-related circumstances. They may not have considered other perspectives and reasons for responding readily to all life experiences that call for forgiving others. When we are gripped and paralyzed by our assumptions, we miss opportunities to understand, appreciate, and accept others for who they are.

It is healthy for the wronged person to forgive the person who wronged them. Ephesians 4:26–27 admonishes us not to allow our anger to become sin. It should be handled expediently.

Matthew 6:14–15 describes a crucial benefit of forgiveness. God will forgive us if we forgive. It keeps us in alignment with God's will. It is beautiful to know that when we sin, which we will, God forgives us and forgets our sins. It is liberating!

I wish the crime and the tragic death of my brother had not happened, but it did. I cannot say that God told me to forgive my brother and the police officer. Again, I did what I saw my parents do in other life experiences that called for forgiveness: they prayed about the situation and for the perpetrator and the person who was wronged. I could have been angry for the rest of my life and allowed my anger to manifest unexpectedly, potentially harming myself and others. Forgiveness was the right thing to do. I could not have done it without God's help. I forgave, and I will not forget. This tragedy is one of my early remembrances of God's nearness and my choice not to forget what he had done. It was a pathway through a difficult time in my life.

STONE OF REMEMBRANCE: REDEMPTION

When I revisited Gregory's death in that police department office, God kept me from carrying hatred or bitterness toward police officers. I couldn't let this tragedy define me. Yet, I do not deny that it happened. God shifted my focus and gave me a different perspective to benefit my community by supporting public servants and making forgiveness possible. God can redeem all things for his glory.

---

3. Van Sant, *Finding Forrester*, 02:12:05–17.

REFLECTION QUESTIONS

In reflecting on your own early childhood memories, what would your story be about? How did a profound impact help shape your beliefs or passions? Did you experience gain or loss? If so, what was it? How did it affect you? What is your stone of remembrance?

3

Oh, Happy Day!

Thank you for being authentically yourself without shame, a challenge many women face. In the end, you ask the audience to take a ride with you in the most personal places in your life, and that, my friend, is brave.
—Idella Posey Winfield

ONE EVENING, A YOUNG man walked toward me from the other side of the room. I was twenty-nine, and it was the mid-eighties. Carl and I worked for different companies and hadn't met before. His pleasant smile caught my attention, and he looked good in a white shirt with black pants, a dark plaid jacket hanging from his shoulders. He gently took my hand as we talked and headed to the dance floor. He tried to impress me, giving me an ear full of how much he liked his work, but neither of us expressed an interest in continuing our conversation or dancing. When the song ended, we thanked each other and walked away.

But Carl's talk had triggered something in me. As I walked back to our table to join my colleagues, I began thinking there must be something more in life than this. At the time, I could not put my finger on what I meant by this or what change I desired. I just realized I wasn't happy at the "happy hour" anymore.

Until then, I had enjoyed hanging out with managers, sales reps, administrators, and technical staff at our gatherings after work on Fridays, where we wound down after a long week at work. We danced, drank, told stories, and ate delicious hors d'oeuvres at an upscale bar named Yesterday's in the Southfield Sheraton Hotel near Detroit. Without our company, that place would not have been as exciting. Our titles and formality were left behind, the suit jackets unbuttoned, and the bows and ties were loosened. It didn't matter if you were single or married; we had fun whether we were there for ten minutes or three hours. It was more than a place to be.

A single woman desiring a professional career over marriage was not unusual in the eighties, as the glass ceiling in places previously dominated by men was being broken. As I think about the image of being "on my own" today, it expresses how I took ownership of my life then.

My heart was set on a career after I earned my bachelor's degree at twenty-nine, and I saw a world of opportunities that I had not been aware of before. I was soon hired as a temp to assist the department secretary of a large computer company. The competitive edge here was nothing like in the public sector, where I'd worked before. I liked the challenging environment, and my supervisor noticed it. Within three months, I was invited to come on board as a full-time, regular employee in the customer service department where we received service calls from computer engineers. I liked working on a team and enjoyed the first-class training and the opportunities for advancement. I learned from incredible, courageous women who were trailblazers in corporate America.

Corporate life was good for me. Within ten months, I was offered a temporary assignment to help design a customer service call center for an unannounced software product in Austin, Texas. I had an expense account and lived in a five-star hotel for three weeks before I rented an apartment. This was my first time traveling to another state on behalf of my employer. I was honored to represent our department, and I enjoyed being on my own. Traveling, living, or eating alone didn't bother me. No one I met remained a stranger.

I was highly motivated after returning to our headquarters in Michigan. I received an award for developing a process to handle engineers' incoming calls, secured computer equipment for a nonprofit board I served on, received regular raises, and was the recipient of a national service award—a fully paid trip to San Diego, attended by recipients from all over the United States. I attributed my success to hard work, a good team, and an excellent manager and sponsor. It was one of the best times in my life and career. I loved life and especially work. It was essential to me. I was loyal to my supervisor, wanting her to be successful.

I had worked various jobs to earn extra money since I was fourteen—from babysitting, ironing shirts for a distant cousin living across the street from us, and working in a daycare center. Because I went to summer school twice, I graduated at sixteen, longing to start working to earn my own salary. Working in a city job was considered safe and secure, and I saved money to get an apartment and a new car and to be able to choose the clothes I wanted. Working gave me a sense of pride and accomplishment. When my father helped me get my first credit card at Sears, Roebuck after graduating high school, I paid my credit balance as soon as the bill came in the mail. I filled my hope chest with colorful linens and other substantial items.

Still, after that experience of walking away from Carl on the dance floor, I kept thinking there had to be something more in life. I wanted more of something, but it was likely not work related.

A couple of years after that experience, I was at a department store one Saturday afternoon in the housewares department. I saw someone I'd seen at Yesterday's, someone from our happy hour. He recognized me also. I knew his name and position in our organization but nothing else. Maybe he knew my name, but we introduced ourselves anyway. Jim invited me for lunch, and I accepted.

We saw each other regularly for two years until God intervened. I'd experienced Jim as calm, intelligent, and reserved. He was slim, tall, dark-brown skinned, and handsome. I enjoyed his love, gentleness, and energy. He complimented me on my appearance, even after long hours at work. He was pleasant to be around, and his language was always appropriate and kind. I saw that our coworkers responded to him with respect, and he was fun to be around. I noticed his self-confidence and that he didn't bring attention to himself. He easily shared what he liked or didn't like about situations. I met some of his family, and he talked about his parents. He was a PK, a preacher's kid, like me. I dearly respected him, and I believe it was mutual.

One evening, Jim and I danced, had a couple of drinks, and played pool until around eight o'clock at a local bar. Both of us had worked a long day, and we always enjoyed spending time together. At one point, we danced to Patti LaBelle and Michael McDonald's song "On My Own," one of the most popular songs of the eighties. I kept singing it in my head.

In "On My Own," the two lovers were brokenhearted over an unexpected breakup, and would be going their separate ways. They didn't understand why their relationship ended this way, and the song doesn't reveal the nature of the breakup. I had experienced breakups and disappointments, but no specific relationship came to mind. Now, though, I can see that the way the song stuck with me might have been a message about my relationship with Jim. My close girlfriends were married or divorced. I had never married; I was on my own, and that was the persona I had created. I was driven by a desire to have a successful career and have influence without necessarily being married, although I'd had two opportunities that could have potentially led to the altar.

As Jim and I walked to the parking lot that evening, he paused and looked into my eyes. I thought we were about to kiss good night.

Instead, he said, "Posie, have you thought about having an intimate, personal relationship with Jesus Christ?"

Surprised, I said, "What?" I did not understand what he was asking me.

"Posie, have you considered having an intimate, personal relationship with Jesus Christ?" he repeated.

I thought about my understanding of what it meant to be a Christian. I was a good person and went to church sometimes and had grown up in the church. I had seen a person in church get happy—moved by the Holy Spirit—although it had never happened to me. I did not fully understand what that person had experienced. I wondered if Jim was referring to that kind of experience. I knew that God existed, and I was sure of God's love for me. I just knew it. Feelings of God's love came over me in small ways and made me smile, and sometimes it brought tears, but Jim was asking me something more, something deeper.

Although I never answered Jim's question, he knew my answer was no. I was too slow trying to come up with an answer.

He said, "Well." Then, "I want you to read two books: *The God You Could Know* by Dan DeHaan and the Gospel of John in the Bible. I'll give you a copy of the book tomorrow. Do you have a Bible?"

"Yes, I have several Bibles."

"Wonderful."

We hugged and said good night. On my drive home, I thought about our strange, unsettling conversation. I had no idea why Jim had asked me about my relationship with God. No one else had ever asked me, and I assumed they thought I was okay in this area or were afraid to ask. Now, I know Jim was being convicted by the Holy Spirit to ask me that simple yet profound and critical question.

Later, I would reflect that Jim's love for me came from the heart of God. He did not try to coerce, embarrass, or scare me into having an encounter with God.

I had kept feeling that something was missing, and later I would realize that I had been seeking to know God. Later still, I learned in the book *The Critical Journey*, by Janet O. Hagberg and Robert A. Guelich, that I was in stage one, "The Recognition of God," in my journey of faith—discovering who God is.[1] I found their book helpful in understanding my spiritual formation. I was grateful for the gentle nudge from Jim to consider Jesus more deeply. As I'd promised, I read the book *The God You Can Know* and the Bible over the next month. My reading was followed by conversations with Jim.

When God became our common interest and desire, I saw that the repetition of the song "On My Own" was awakening me to the fact that Jim's and my relationship was inappropriate for reasons I'm not free to explain, except to say that God was not honored by it. Surprisingly, our romantic relationship was not difficult for me to let go of because I had clearly come to understand that a greater power was at work, and I knew God was steering this ship.

I read in 1 Cor 7:34, "The unmarried woman or virgin is concerned about the Lord's affairs: Her aim is to be devoted to the Lord in both body and spirit." I was gripped by the phrases "concerned about the Lord's affairs" and "devoted to the Lord in both body and spirit." With those words, my feelings for Jim changed quickly. The words had fallen on good soil.

DeHaan's book taught me what it is like when a heart is set on knowing God. It's incredible. Our love grows greater, and we are motivated by that love. I began to realize that I had been seeking love not in God but in my career and male companionship. God is love, and he is a jealous God. He is the source of our love and wants to be our love's object. I had been living my life according to Denise. Temporal things do not result in "stability, security, and understanding in doing God's will," according to DeHaan.[2]

One of the crucial things I learned from *The God You Can Know* was that God created us to know and enjoy him. I kept reading to discover why this was not happening in my life. I was curious to know what was missing and longing to know what needed to change. I was about to find out.

---

1. Hagberg and Guelich, *Critical Journey*, 33.
2. DeHaan, *God You Can Know*, 13.

God awakened me one morning at three o'clock, and I turned on the radio. It was already set on a Christian station. I heard, "Stay tuned to Power for Deliverance Ministry with your host, Pastor Michael Keith." The theme song was "Until You Make It Through" by Candi Staton. I did not know what I was about to go through, and I would not have been able to do it on my own, which I was so accustomed to. God was speaking to me through Staton's words: "But I was reaching my hand out to you, offering my love, to you, saying child, I'll help you through." It was prophetic. I knew the Lord was speaking to me about what I needed, and he would help me.

I experienced the tenderness of God's love. Later I would realize that he knew I was looking for meaning in life, because he put the desire in my heart. I had been looking for love in the wrong places. I knew something was going to happen but didn't know what and when. I still did not know that I needed healing from my past, that I was broken. But God, even then, wanted me to grasp how wide and long and high and deep is the love of Christ, that I was not alone. There was a holy presence in the room, which made me feel like everything would be made right, as I listened to the song.

This awakening continued at the same time—three o'clock in the morning—for about three weeks, to plant God's message in my heart as I repeatedly listened to "Until You Make It Through." The words evoked gratitude and tears. I will never forget how God reached out to me. Even today, sometimes, those words from Staton's song come to mind, and they comfort me. God continues cultivating a loving relationship, reminding me that I am his child no matter what happens, and he loves me.

One day after work, I parked my car in the garage and entered the house through the back door as usual. My life was about to change forever. I stepped into the kitchen and closed the door. When I went into the dining room, I was overwhelmed by a holy presence. I knew it was the presence of the Lord. I was not afraid but in awe. I dropped my briefcase on the floor as I was drawn to get down on my knees. I looked up and cried, "I need you to save me, Lord." My plea to Jesus came from deep within and from a sense of desperation. I wanted Jesus. Every time I tried to stop crying, the tears flowed again.

Then I had a conscious awareness of my sins. I repeatedly cried, "Lord, I'm sorry." I was sorry it took so long for me to hear his voice and recognize his hand in my life. "Lord, forgive my sins and cleanse me of my unrighteousness. I need you." Psalm 51:17 describes my posture: "My sacrifice, O God, is a broken spirit; a broken and contrite heart you, God, will not despise." I knew God did not bring me this far to leave me hanging. He says in Heb 10:22, "Let us draw near to God with a sincere heart and with the full assurance that faith brings, having our hearts sprinkled to cleanse us from a guilty conscience and having our bodies washed with pure water." I was guilty, but my shame had been undone.

At that moment, my whole self was like an open book before God. He knew more about me than I could know about myself. I felt vulnerable and naked before the Almighty God, not condemned but fully loved by my Creator. I felt my Father's smile as he wrapped his loving arms around his prodigal daughter. He never left me, though I had left him years before.

I was freed, rescued, and restored. I could no longer live to and for myself. I belonged to Jesus, and I was part of the faith community. I received God's amazing grace. Satan would no longer have a stronghold over my life. I surrendered and offered myself to the Lord. I wanted God to reign in my life. Immediately, I no longer wanted to live as I had done in the past. I was freed from my yesterdays. I had read about the work of the Spirit in the Gospel of John, and I wanted to live in the Spirit, not the flesh. I knew I would not be able to make it through without the Helper. I phoned Jim, and we gave God praise for his goodness.

Years later, I thought about how Joseph's brothers sold him to the Egyptian merchants to get rid of him, but God meant it for good. When I initially met Jim in the department store, Satan meant it for evil. As I thought about it later, God knew who I would receive his message from and how. I saw that the Holy Spirit had brought God's love to me through Jim, *The God You Can Know*, and "Until You Make It Through."

Sometime after my conversion experience, I attended a worship service and heard the visiting preacher talk about his friend, Dan DeHaan, the author of *The God You Can Know*. He had been an incredible youth minister. He was a graduate of Columbia International University, formerly Columbia Bible College in South Carolina. On February 19, 1982, Dan was killed when the plane he was flying crashed. He was just thirty-three years old. Although Dan was with his Lord, others were brought into God's kingdom through his witness.[3] God used his book in my life in 1988, six years after his death. Dan's friend was deeply moved when I told him my story.

I had been looking for something only God could give, and he intervened and gave me what I was seeking—meaning for my life. I was not my

---

3. Speed, "Dan DeHaan," 23.

own, nor was I on my own. I later found language for that in the Heidelberg Catechism:

> *What is your only comfort in life and in death?*
> That I am not my own, but belong—body and soul,
> in life and in death—to my faithful Savior, Jesus Christ.
> He has fully paid for all my sins with his precious blood,
> and has set me free from the tyranny of the devil. He also watches over me in such a way that not a hair can fall from my head without the will of my Father in heaven; in fact, all things must work together for my salvation.
>
> Because I belong to him, Christ, by his Holy Spirit,
> assures me of eternal life and makes me wholeheartedly willing
> and ready from now on to live for him.[4]

My conversion story is as real today as it was when it happened. When I share my story, I experience the intensity of that moment. I will not forget it.

In the New Testament, the apostle Paul recalled and shared his Damascus Road conversion story with the disciples in Damascus, the apostles in Jerusalem, and the Roman officials as he was bound in chains. He never forgot. These memories were so much a part of who he was. Geoffrey Cubitt notes our memories are a part of our very existence, and if we deprive ourselves of them, we risk our sense of personal identity.[5]

When a person's present experience triggers something from their past, they are intensely aware of that memory because of their self-knowing. They do not just know about the memory; they reexperience the memory. A significant happening was acted upon an individual. They actually lived an experience; they were not bystanders.[6]

I shared my God encounter with my friend Cosette the next day at work. She said, "Thank you, Jesus! I've been praying for you. You haven't received everything; there is more." A young male colleague, Ivy, said, "Posie, I'm so happy for you." I waited for my friend Shirley to finish her customer call to tell her. Her face lit up. She said, "Praise the Lord!" Jesus' light was shining through for others to see. The joy of the Lord was in me.

My sisters later told me they had noticed a difference in me, although their responses were different. They saw a change in my attitude. I was more

---

4. Christian Reformed Church, "Heidelberg Catechism," Q&A 1.
5. Cubitt, *History and Memory*, 66
6. Cubitt, *History and Memory*, 67.

pleasant than before, not so uppity. I knew God had changed me. Even when I walked away from him, he was molding and shaping me. I could not imagine the depth of his love until I had that experience in my dining room. God changed the trajectory of my life so I would follow Jesus and let go of worldliness. I believe he will do the same for others.

I knew there would be more for me. It was a new beginning. Praise God for his goodness!

STONE OF REMEMBRANCE: SALVATION

I'll never forget the freedom I experienced the day Jesus set me free! Remembering my own conversion experience has allowed me to be available to the Holy Spirit as God draws others who are looking for meaning in life to himself. "For God so loved the world, that he gave his only Son, that whoever believes in him should not perish but have eternal life" (John 3:16).

REFLECTION QUESTIONS

At what point in life did you receive Jesus Christ as your Lord and Savior? What effect did it have on you and others at the time? Think about a time when you shared your story with someone else. What were the circumstances and how were you impacted? What is your stone of remembrance?

4

Seven Years Were Enough

Recognizing God is a prerequisite to experiencing his goodness and remembering what he has done in our lives.
—Janet Thompson

Although I had met internal monthly goals and customer satisfaction in my role at a major computer company, I had felt unfulfilled for the past six months. In 1990, a couple of years after my decision to follow Jesus wholeheartedly, managing receivable accounts for major customers' equipment purchases in the marketing unit was no longer meeting my needs. I had an unsettledness about my work. I wanted more customer engagement, travel, and fewer administrative details that kept me tied to my desk.

I imagined myself in a sales rep position, meeting quotas and solving customer problems by exploring and finding solutions to meet their needs. It would give me a greater challenge, mobility, visibility, and fulfillment. The thought of making sales in marketing was intriguing. The earning potential was attractive, although I was not hungry for a six-figure salary. In my two years in accounts receivable in the marketing department, I always sat in the front row in our departmental meetings to cheer on the sales reps and embrace their moments of accomplishment, which I longed to be a part of.

The time came when I decided to take a chance and make the switch from receivables to sales. I had heard stories about how difficult it was for blacks to thrive in sales for the long haul. Retention was one of the problems. It kept the company from reaching a double-digit percentage for racial diversity in our region. A sales rep could be here today and gone tomorrow. One day you realize you haven't seen a rep for a while, and someone says they are no longer here, without knowing the backstory.

Our executive staff consisted of at least one or two tried and proven, longtime black sales managers. Black people in technical and administrative positions outnumbered sales reps relative to the overall number of employees in the marketing unit, which wasn't unusual.

Within three weeks of my inquiry and pretest for the sales rep position, I felt some resistance from my potential team manager, Janice. I asked, "What is your response? Will I be able to join your team as a sales rep?"

With a smile, she said, "Yes," like a parent telling their daughter not to try something because they knew she would not get the results she hoped for.

When the time came for the announcement meeting, my coworkers stood on the sidelines, optimistically clapping and cheering me on. It gave me an extra boost for the move to a new level of expectations, responsibilities, and competition. I recall praying about this move and did not sense a warning to stop. I stepped through the door when it finally opened.

I got situated in the condo with my classmates in Atlanta. I enjoyed meeting my peers on our first day of our marketing class. I felt and saw a combination of joy and anxiety beneath our casual business attire and bright, shining faces. We carried with us the weight of studying and preparing for long hours and days before our arrival. Classes would be long and have few breaks.

About six months after my first sales class, I was overwhelmingly challenged by the second class. I sat in a small, isolated room at work, reading a manual on the internal components of computers and copiers and how they work. I felt reluctant and nervous about making an upcoming presentation. My confidence level was low, unlike in the first class about customer engagement. I don't like getting caught up in the details. I wasn't getting very far with understanding this technical but important material. I pressed on.

Perhaps if I had the support of a mentor or sponsor, I would have benefitted from check-ins and strategies for dealing with learning challenges. It is difficult to navigate new terrain when you do not have someone to walk alongside you for emotional and professional support and access to resources. You either swim or drown. That's just the way it was. The water current exceeded my safety zone. My reputation and previous accomplishments for six years in our organization meant less in marketing. I was expected to prove myself, but I questioned whether I could make it through successfully. Today, I wonder, "Why didn't I ask for help?" All the courses were comprehensive and intensive. Previous students had said, "It's like drinking water from a fire hydrant." It was.

At the end of the two-week training, there was a sigh of relief when we received our scores. I did not finish well. At this point, I wondered if it was time for me to leave the company. I dreaded meeting with Janice the following week, but I had to face this challenge. We met on Monday morning. When she asked how the class went, I responded, "I didn't pass."

Her mouth dropped, and she gave me two options: "Retake the course or return to your previous administrative position." If I retook the course, it was with the stipulation that I score at least the class average to remain in the training program.

Frankly, I was surprised I had options. I was not ready to give her an answer, but I appreciated a few extra days before I had to let her know. I rarely make critical decisions without seeking godly counsel and prayer.

I made an appointment with my pastor, the late Rev. Dr. Frederick G. Sampson II of Tabernacle Missionary Baptist Church in Detroit, the next day. The twenty-minute drive to church was pleasant as I listened to worship music and prayed. I was greeted by Dr. Sampson at his office door. In the black church, going to the pastor's office is like going to the principal's office in school when you've done something wrong. Other than his exceptional preaching and teaching, Tabernacle members appreciated his pastoral heart, wisdom, humility, and discernment. Sometimes a discerning pastor knows when one of their sheep is going through a difficult situation, even when there are no external signs.

We sat at a small conference table facing each other. After asking how I was doing, Dr. Sampson reached for my hands to pray for the Holy Spirit to guide our conversation. After praying in Jesus' name, he looked and said, "All right."

I explained why I left administration for sales. I mentioned the two options.

"Do you want to return to the administrative position?"

"No."

"Do you want to retake the marketing class?"

"Yes, and I want to know God's will. I have never been a quitter and don't want to return to my previous position." If I went back, I felt like I would be boxed in with no room for growth and advancement. I could not play it safe just for the sake of having a job, but I had never left any job without a plan.

My pastor, church family, and friends knew God had his hand on me. I did too. There was this burning desire to know God and his plan for my life. Dr. Sampson held my hands firmly as he closed our meeting in prayer. "I want to meet again after you see what God is doing in this situation." He had joined this journey with me, and I felt supported.

After returning to work, I told Janice I would retake the class.

"Go for it!" she said.

I was encouraged by her response. I did not expect it to be easier this time, but I stayed optimistic.

I enjoyed getting to know new classmates from various states. It was a bonus when I was elected as the class president. That warranted a note or phone call to your manager. I sent this fantastic news in a message to Janice.

After the two-week training, we were given our final scores and certificates of completion. The class average was seventy-eight, and I scored seventy-six. I was so close, but close was not what we had agreed upon. At this point, I recognized my dilemma as an opportunity for God's intervention. I didn't think the door to marketing would remain open.

Later I phoned three colleagues who knew me well and had my best interest in mind. They told me not to quit. It was important to hear their voices as part of making my decision. I called Mildred, a team manager in the customer service department who knew my work history well. I accepted an invitation to join her for a conversation when I returned to the Detroit area. Then, I called Janice to let her know about my course grade, and she said, "You know what this means."

"Yes."

"We will discuss it sometime after you return to the office next week. Have a good weekend."

It took every bit of God's strength in me to ward off lingering thoughts of defeat, shame, or not being good enough. I counted on God to see me through. Still, I had fun with my classmates until we gave hearty hugs and goodbyes at the airport and went our separate ways to take flights home. I left, not knowing if we would meet again in the next training class.

I met with Mildred in the customer service department on Monday. I appreciated her concern and invitation for me to stop by her office, which was in a different building from mine. Her words were strong.

"Your manager is walking on a thin sheet of ice. They don't have grounds to fire you because you did pass the course." According to her, it didn't make any difference that I was two points below the average score.

"In the upcoming meeting, use marketing terms and point out being elected as class president. That was outstanding." She told me to let them know about my strengths and weaknesses. "You're self-aware."

I listened intently.

"Do not waiver," she added.

We hugged, and I left. I appreciated having an experienced woman in leadership coach me in asserting myself.

One senior-level male manager in another branch said, "If I were ever put on the frontline, I would want you as my leader. You have more guts than I have."

"I do not know why, but I must go through it."

I was not encouraged by another colleague's remarks. "I thought you said God blessed you with the marketing position."

"Yes, that's right."

"When God blesses you, he makes you successful."

"Yes, but he does not look at success from a worldly perspective."

"How unfortunate."

That was the end of our conversation. I thought, "He just doesn't understand God's ways." I knew God's hand was on this situation as I walked in his peace that surpasses all understanding. I would not let what someone else said about me become my issue. Instead, I asked, "Lord, did you bring me this far to leave me? Show me what you want me to learn from this situation."

On Tuesday, before falling asleep at two in the morning, I was blessed by the words in a song on the radio, "I'll be with you because I am the Lord. Just put your trust in me. I'll be right by your side." I repeatedly remembered and said aloud, "I'll be with you." Then I closed my eyes to sleep. I slept well.

On Wednesday morning, I reached out to my training advisor in Atlanta. She told me they had not given Janice any indication that I could not make it as a sales rep. "Do not give in so quickly, and take ownership," she said. That was excellent advice.

My appointment with Janice was late in the morning. I had requested a meeting with Gary, the marketing branch manager and Janice's manager. When I arrived at the office, Janice knew of my request to meet with him.

Several team managers were assigned to industries/accounts, and there was one marketing branch manager, Gary. I liked his personality, wisdom, presence, and strong corporate acumen. In hindsight, I should have checked with Janice to see if meeting with Gary was all right with her. She politely let me know the next step. "If you want to see him, you should go now and return later."

I walked a few feet down the hallway to his office. I kept my cool and respectfully stood my ground. I took responsibility for my decisions and failure to meet Janice's expectations. I didn't break.

He couldn't understand why I wanted to continue in this capacity. "Why don't you want to give it up?"

Finally, I said, "I cannot quit." As far as I was concerned, this was the only position I desired and would work hard for. I enjoyed helping customers solve problems and meeting their needs. I wanted to contribute to a winning team and earn a higher salary. "The training material was difficult, but I learned more the second time," I added.

He offered options: "I can release you; you can quit; you can go back to administration; or you can continue in the program."

He would be unlikely to choose the fourth option, based on my test score. We continued. It boiled down to the investment, dollars spent on me by the company—two hundred thousand. Gary said, "We want you to finish the training program as quickly as possible."

I understood the concern. "I cannot quit."

"You have to put yourself in my shoes."

I tilted my head slightly as our eyes made contact. I thought, "You should put yourself in my shoes." He would decide the next day.

Janice stopped by my cubicle. I was surprised because we were scheduled to meet in her office. I looked up as she stood in front of me with one arm resting on the top of my cubicle. I stood up. She looked directly into my eyes with her arms folded. "I don't understand why you're doing this to yourself. It's like Saddam Hussein was willing to die before he would back down, then he got to a point where he had to give up. You wouldn't be a successful rep even if you made it through the training."

"I would be successful if I had good support," I said. I was never asked what kind of support I would need.

"At some point, you have to give up."

I agreed. "I have not reached that point yet."

She nodded, kept her head down, and walked away with a slight smile.

I thought, "You just don't understand."

I felt like I had been beaten like a punching bag as I left the office. Marketing has a reputation for being cutthroat. Why wasn't one small ounce of hope possible?

The next day I would go to meet my fate. That night I slept well, took a walk in the morning, showered, ate breakfast, and put on a navy blue suit and white blouse. I bowed my head and prayed briefly, sitting on the couch before leaving home. I prayed for God's will to be done. Within seconds I heard him say, "Do not be surprised when you are fired." He said *when*, not *if*. These words strengthened me. I am an optimist, so I needed to understand the seriousness of this encounter. He would bring me out of corporate. I understood that God had the power to open and close doors. I was not in control of my own life. God is omnipresent, omnipotent, and omniscient. This was not a failure on my part or anyone else's part. The outcome was God's will, not my will. In the future, when doors opened or closed, I would remember this spiritual encounter to help me accept God's will. I knew that the outcome of my meeting with Gary would result in what God had already told me.

As usual, I left for a fifteen-minute drive to the office with my head up, in professional attire. I always dressed for success. I paused and then knocked on Gary's open door before entering. I called his name, and he politely asked me to sit down and wanted to know how I was doing.

I barely smiled. "I'm doing well."

The ball was in his court. My destiny had already been decided, and I knew he would choose to release me. I knew who really had control over my future. Gary began by saying lovely things about my personality, work ethic, and character. He told me how difficult this decision was for him.

I wished I'd asked, "What do you mean?" I was still relaxed in anticipation of his decision. He did not know I was prayerfully remembering what God had told me about my fate. My soul was well because I remembered what God had already said.

"Your employment will end immediately," he said emotionally, leaning back in his seat with his head slightly down and hands clasped in front of him, resting on his lap. His eyes looked somewhat teary.

My lips tightened before my delayed response. "All right," I said and stood.

Then he stood. His response was genuine; I knew he felt terrible about making this decision. At that moment, I knew it was not God's will for me to continue this path in the corporate sector.

I turned and hugged him. "I will be all right," I said. I left. It was a bittersweet moment.

I returned to my desk with an escort to briefly say goodbye and give a thumbs-up to my colleagues. I quickly turned in my keys, identification badge, and credit card. I released the things that gave me status and a sense of empowerment. I felt the loss. In those days, having an American Express card and a travel expense account were prestigious. It felt like a turning point. God was teaching me to surrender again. My success would no longer be determined by my will, amenities, and external circumstances but by doing God's will. I did not know yet what that was, but it was not in corporate.

Hagberg and Guelich helped me understand what I was going through. In what is called "The Journey Inward," stage four, God interrupts our lives to get our attention. He takes us through a process to determine whether we will surrender to his will and guidance. The authors note the difficulty of putting words to this divine, personalized experience. "Fundamentally, it has to do with slowly breaking down barriers we have built between our will and a newer awareness of God in our lives."[1] Stage four is also referred to as "The Wall."

A person may approach the Wall in their life journey once or continuously. The Wall can be a transformative experience if we yield to the Spirit's guidance. The Wall represents our will as it meets God's will. It represents how we live before God shakes our sense of purpose and security. He uses the process to break our will. It means dying to self and producing a harvest, as described in the Gospel of John 12:24: "Very truly I tell you, unless a kernel of wheat falls to the ground and dies, it remains only a single seed. But if it dies, it produces many seeds."

The process carries us through four phases: awareness of our blind spots, forgiveness of ourselves and others, acceptance of "all" of who we are, and love for ourselves, God, and others. We experience "God's love that heals our lives, calms our egos, soothes our chaotic wills into submission, and lets God direct our lives."[2] Unfortunately, not everyone decides to go through the Wall for various reasons. In my situation, I was willing to go

1. Hagberg and Guelich, *Critical Journey*, 114.
2. Hagberg and Guelich, *Critical Journey*, 114–15.

through it, and my willingness relates to my conversion experience. I did not know how to name what God was taking me through until years later.

The entire experience becomes memorable and important in subsequent situations that require following Jesus through difficult places and times. For instance, I recalled a conversation that had a profound effect on me.

Thomas, a coworker, and I had briefly conversed while passing each other in the hall.

He asked, "Have you heard anything yet?"

I said, "No, I'm still waiting."

"To get ahead, you must go to your manager and demand what you want. You must be a complainer to get a promotion."

"No, I am waiting to see what God's will is. I want to do things God's way. I'm still waiting on the Lord."

What my coworker suggested is exactly what shouldn't happen as we go through the Wall. Instead, God taught me that I could trust him to provide for "all my needs." God chose to teach me this truth early in my faith formation. He taught me how to receive from him. The thought of receiving from God deeply touched me because I was previously accustomed to getting what I needed or wanted on my own. Multiple entries in my journal suggest I was open to God's will, without demanding anything. God would show himself to always be faithful in providing for all my needs.

I will fight in God's strength and Spirit for what he wants for me or someone else, if necessary. I'm not being confrontational to get what I want, as my coworker had suggested, but I do fight for things, knowing that this is God's way and trusting that the battle is not mine but God's.

I went to church that Wednesday night directly from work, as usual. Upon entering the lower-level fellowship hall, I met Sister Bond, a beautifully gray-haired senior with a lovely spirit and warmth.

"Denise, you are glowing," she said.

I thought about how the external reflects the soul. "I just lost my job."

"No!"

Before she said anything else, I blurted out, "I feel good, though!"

She knew the nature of my work based on previous conversations. She smiled, and we went our separate ways.

I imagined feeling like Moses in Exod 34 when he came down from Mount Sinai after being in the Lord's presence, when he didn't know his face was glowing. I had a God encounter when I was praying before I left my house to meet with Gary, and God said, "Do not be surprised when you are fired." These words anchored my soul. It was well with my soul, and my face was radiant with his glory. I was ready to worship God for who he is and what he had done for me in bringing me through a difficult, crucial moment in my life.

I sat in the second row in the fellowship hall as usual. On the way to my seat, someone else told me how beautiful I looked. As Christians, we "are being transformed into his [the Lord's] image with ever-increasing glory, which comes from the Lord, who is the Spirit," as stated in 2 Cor 3:18. Our beauty, the glory of the Lord, comes from the Spirit, and it manifests on the outside. It's noticeable. It did not come from me. It came from the Lord.

My pastor was the only one in the church who knew the whole story about losing my job. I had been taught to not leave a secure position until I had another one lined up. I went against one of my own principles, but it would not be God's last strategic move.

We sang hymns and prayed. During personal testimonies, I shared my story about losing my job. But I didn't take this lightly. It was a sad day in some ways but also a joyful completion of my assignment in corporate America, a *jubilee moment* for me. I do not remember if I cried. If so, they were tears of joy. I accepted God's invitation to move forward into the next phase of my life, launching into the unknown with his unconditional love, peace, and promises.

STONE OF REMEMBRANCE: PEACE

Remembering what God had told me the morning I lost my job gave me peace because God revealed his will for me. I experienced Phil 4:7: "And the peace of God, which transcends all understanding, will guard your hearts and your minds in Christ Jesus." Sometimes, God will prepare us for something that would normally rock our world if we had not been prepared.

REFLECTION QUESTIONS

Recall a time when you received a word or message from God when the stakes were high. How did it help you understand and receive God's hand at work in your spiritual formation? What did you learn about God? What is your stone of remembrance?

5

Launching into the Unknown

> Sanctification takes place ultimately to spread God's glory, which is our primary mission. —Marny Köstenberger

After a whirlwind year in marketing, there was room to exhale and slowly breathe fresh air as I joined the unemployed population. I was ready to experience God's ways, in a new rhythm of life, but I didn't have any set expectations. My heart was open though.

I was off to a good start when I decided to visit my parents' house the day after losing my job. Dad had gone to the store. Mom surprised me. After hearing what had happened, she told me to sit on the bed beside her. I will never forget this moment because my mom and I had often clashed. After all, we were both strong-willed.

She said, "You must find out what you want to do next." She knew how much my work meant to me. I listened as a daughter seeking to receive wisdom from her mother. It felt good to allow her to be my mom at this critical moment of uncertainty. I told her I'd take it easy for a while. She didn't put any pressure on me to find a job. I felt loved and cared for, as I let myself be vulnerable, unlike in past experiences. I had to let go of my desire to have answers and a plan.

To myself, I wondered if I would embrace this new season or long for the past. Fortunately, I did not have many bills. My mortgage payment was the most critical. Still, there was a lot I didn't know about my future.

God had given me hope in my time of uncertainty. About a year earlier, in my quiet time with the Lord, I had prayed a daily prayer recommended by Dr. Charles Stanley, a radio pastor, about putting on the whole armor of God, based on Eph 6:10–17. It included, "I put on this helmet that will protect my mind from any negative thoughts, doubt, and fear. I choose to stop every impure and negative thought at the door of my mind." This gave me great comfort and courage. The prayer was right on time; more than ever, I wanted to guard against negativity distracting me from what was important, especially during this season. I didn't want to be afraid to do new things. It was a beginning for me with many unknowns.

It was a fresh start in praying differently than I had before. I wrote in my journal at the time, "My heart cries out to you, Lord. Show me your way. Each day, I want to grow closer and closer to you. I will love you with all my heart, all my soul, all my mind, and with all my strength. This is my heart's greatest desire." This was my vow and cry unto the Lord, that I would love him from the depth of my soul because he saved me from my sins. This was a new longing for me. I didn't sound like the woman who wanted to be on her own anymore. I belonged to God, his beloved child, and he waited for me.

Consequently, I resolved to live as a single woman honoring God in both body and soul, as a form of surrender to his will.

It would be important for me to study the Bible in community with women so that we could share openly and support each other as sisters journeying with Jesus. Most of us were single at the time.

I had planned for a weekly home Bible study several weeks before I left my job. Norma, Gwen, Lonetta, Cosette, Liz, and Naomi came over after work to join me around my dining room table to study the upcoming Sunday school lesson and pray, for three years. There were usually three to five women each week. We always had situations in our own lives to apply the lesson.

One day, to their surprise, I shared with Norma and Gwen a short praise song that came to me while I was in the shower. I wrote these words in my journal later:

> In the midst of all his blessings, I'm going to praise the Lord.
> In the midst of all his blessings, I'm going to praise the name of Jesus.
> In the midst of tribulations, I'm going to praise the Lord.
> In the midst of tribulations, I'm going to praise the name of Jesus.
> Oh, God, you've been so good to me.
> In the midst of tribulations,
> I'm going to praise the name of Jesus.

Gwen said, "I've never heard that one. It's a beautiful testimony." I remember this little praise song, today, when I need to encourage myself in the Lord. It is a reminder to praise God all the time because he is good. I knew God was changing me. I would not have expressed myself this way in the past. Yes, it is a beautiful testimony that my soul is well, even when I can't know or see my way forward.

Oswald Chambers says in the sanctification process, eventually, our walk in Christ aligns with our faith. Sometimes God orchestrates circumstances that lead us to where theory and our walk of faith align. "Once we get there, no matter where God places us or what the inner desolations are, we can praise God that all is well."[1]

One time, Naomi shared her story about being entangled in a relationship and having sex after being celibate for many years. Previously, she had boasted to her friends about her choice to be celibate. Shortly after that, she found herself unable to resist sexual temptation. She slipped and expressed how disappointed she was with herself. We assured her that none of us is perfect; she wasn't going to get pounced on by us. We encouraged her to receive God's forgiveness and put on the whole armor of God as described in Eph 6. Sometimes, we ask God to forgive us, but we carry a load of guilt and shame because we cannot forgive ourselves. Sometimes, we allow our flesh or Satan to convince us that we aren't forgiven, and we don't experience God's grace and mercy.

I never thought I would go down a similar road myself two years later. I found myself in a vulnerable situation with a man while visiting my friend Rita in Illinois. I hadn't met him before, although we knew about each other through our mutual friend. She had known Michael in their youth. They came to pick me up from the airport, and we went out for breakfast. We laughed, joked, and talked about life experiences. Michael and I had a mutual attraction brewing like a good cup of coffee. He was both handsome and charming. Michael was what women would call a ladies' man. He knew what buttons to push to give a woman plenty of attention.

When Rita saw our friendliness, she laughed. "You had better watch out."

I assumed she didn't want me to fall for him, thinking it wouldn't be good for me. I was enjoying myself. We continued to laugh and talk about life and each other. When it was time to leave and go our separate ways, Michael extended his hand.

---

1. Chambers, *My Utmost for His Highest*, 68.

"Bye, Denise," he said.

I said, "I wanna hug." He got closer and gave me one.

Michael stopped by the next day. Enthralled by his conversation, I hardly noticed the time. We were flirting and made plans to get together the next day for lunch. He came by and stood talking with Rita in the living room while I was in the bedroom, teetering between going with Michael or staying at Rita's house. I struggled, and then I knew it needed to stop.

I came from the bedroom to say hello. I was solemn and quiet. Rita and Michael looked at each other and probably wondered what had happened.

I had remembered God bringing me out of my inappropriate relationship with Jim. Still, Satan was on an assignment to steal, kill, or destroy me. He no longer had a stronghold over me. Jesus had set me free. I decided not to go with Michael. I went back to my bedroom and left Michael and Rita standing there. I counted on Michael to accept my decision. He left shortly afterward without a hug or handshake.

I thank God for my victory. It helps to understand our struggles. "For the flesh desires what is contrary to the Spirit, and the Spirit what is contrary to the flesh. They are in conflict with each other, so that you are not to do whatever you want" (Gal 5:17).

I entrusted a letter to Rita to give to Michael after I left to return to Michigan. In the letter, I expressed my attraction to him but told him I couldn't go down that road again. I did not see Michael during the rest of my stay, and I returned to Michigan a few days later. It turned out that we had no further communication.

Right after that, I heard a sermon on the radio about temptation. The preacher said, "We must make a choice. Yea or nay. When this happens, we should rely on Scripture to resist temptation." I knew that I wasn't the person I used to be; I was a new creation (2 Cor 5:17). In God's sanctification process, we become alive to what pleases God and die daily to sin. Unlike before, I had a consciousness and conviction that a relationship with Michael was wrong. I understood my weakness and my strength. Sometimes, we understand our weakness, but we don't understand that our strength comes from God and the power of his word.

Sexual attraction and temptation happen to everyday people. Anyone who plays it down is living on another planet. It can be ignored by single, divorced, and married individuals to their spiritual detriment. Sometimes, we do not talk about it or think it could happen to us. In my circles, we don't talk about it. I'm sorry about Naomi's fall into temptation, but, looking back, hearing her story in our Bible study made me aware of my own vulnerability.

When I have opportunities to meet with women, both young and mature, who have past or current desires or struggles with physical attraction and/or sexual temptation, I try to be compassionate and empathetic. I do not act or want them to act as if physical attraction and/or sexual temptation don't exist or are never on our minds. I will share my story of deliverance and God's goodness to me. Creating a safe, courageous space for these kinds of discussions is rare; however, they are needed. One of my most significant learnings was that victory comes in the Spirit's power, not in my strength. It can be celebrated by giving God the glory.

Through prayer, I committed as an unmarried woman to being "concerned about the Lord's affairs" (1 Cor 7:34). I would honor God by living in alignment with his word. If this meant that I would be celibate for the rest of my life, I was content with that.

As part of the sanctification process, one evening while I was praying, the Holy Spirit led me to anoint myself with oil in the name of the Father, the Son, and the Holy Spirit. I lay on my back in front of the fireplace on the living room floor and anointed myself from the bottoms of my feet to the top of my head with olive oil that I had prayed over. I understood this act of worship was setting me apart for sacrificial service. A pastor once said in his sermon, "Sacrificial service is the outward living of the inward living of the Holy Spirit."

As I understand it today, I was brought to a place of holiness, being set apart. I didn't have a book or guide to instruct me or say whether I had appropriately offered myself or should or shouldn't do it. I knew the Holy Spirit led me, and I was called to God's work. This was the answer I had been waiting for.

I understand this offering within the context of Rom 12:1, "Therefore, I urge you, brothers and sisters, in view of God's mercy, to offer your bodies as a living sacrifice, holy and pleasing to God—this is your true and proper worship." This offering was an entry to doing the Lord's work and living in obedience according to his will, something we are all called to do and be.

I had the privilege of going to Nassau, in the Bahamas, with a delegation from my church for three consecutive summers to teach children and attend a Bible college. On the second trip, I sat next to a female Bahamian pastor who was a few years older than me. The church van picked us up from the hotel to take us to a Bible college to attend classes. I do not remember the context of our conversation, but she shared her own anointing experience. We bowed our heads and gasped in agreement. I said, "Me too." For both of us, it was an affirming, sacred, and holy-ground experience. After my Bahamas experience, I knew change was coming, quicker than I thought.

One Sunday, I had a surprise visit to my Baptist church from Bill, my friend and spiritual companion. I was quite pleased and comfortable at my neighborhood church because it had a good pastor, biblical teaching, choir, and discipleship gatherings. Later, after visiting a few times, Bill convinced me to visit his church, Tabernacle Missionary Baptist Church. It had good teaching and preaching, Bible study classes, theology classes, choirs, and various ministries and fellowship options. The worship service and preaching were aired on the radio every Sunday. Bill's efforts paid off, and I joined Tabernacle and grew to love my church family. Later, I understood the reason why I needed to leave my former church. I would not have been able to fulfill God's calling based on theological differences if I had stayed there.

Tabernacle Church was where I would grow spiritually and bear much fruit. I felt I was on God's accelerated path to oneness with him. I helped myself to a smorgasbord of options to expand my understanding of God, myself, others, and creation. I longed to become more like Jesus. Later, I had learned my longing aligned with writer Robert Mulholland's "fourfold definition of spiritual formation as a process of being formed in the image of Christ for the sake of others."[2] I had experienced "being the subject who controls all other things to being a person who is shaped by the presence, purpose and power of God in all things."[3] Before my conversion, I knew Jesus' love, but I wasn't learning how to be more like him—I was lacking discipleship and spiritual formation. There was much more to learn and become. At the time, I was in "a time of learning and belonging," as noted in stage two, "The Life of Discipleship," in *The Critical Journey*.[4]

On Sundays, I, along with over fifty members and others from local churches, came to a six thirty in the morning Dawn Seekers class where Dr. Sampson, the pastor, taught theology for an hour. Then, I attended the eight o'clock and eleven o'clock morning worship services most Sundays. I was hungry for God's word. Sometimes, after our eleven o'clock morning service, we attended an afternoon service when Dr. Sampson was the guest

2. Mulholland, *Invitation*, 19.
3. Mulholland, *Invitation*, 33.
4. Hagberg and Guelich, *Critical Journey*, 53.

preacher, and we would go out for a meal afterwards with several members. Dr. Sampson loved sharing stories about his family, life, and the Bible at the dinner table. His stories always opened my eyes to a lifetime of God's love and grace.

I was privileged to sit under Dr. Sampson's preaching and teaching for ten years while I lived in Detroit. He had so much to give. I kept my pen and notebook ready because he consistently gave us the meat of God's word in and out of the pulpit. He poured God's wisdom into our lives. Evidence of his intimate relationship with God showed up in many ways, mainly how he treated all people with love and kindness, even if it was not reciprocated. I learned through his faithfulness to God, family, and congregants. He was also prophetic.

One Sunday afternoon several people were talking, following an afternoon service where Dr. Sampson was the revivalist. He came over to us and said, "When the Holy Spirit has you, you have no control." Brother and Sister Bond and Deacon and Sister Robertson and I listened. As he was talking, he was looking at me. He told them that he had told me some time ago that the Holy Spirit had me and that I wanted to know him (referring to God).

He said, "He's got you, and it's just a matter of time."

I didn't know or ask what he meant.

I longed to receive more of whatever God wanted me to have. In my spirit, I knew there was more.

On my first trip to the Bahamas, our church delegation had attended an outdoor worship service at the Bible college. I was sitting with a few women Bible teachers from our church toward the back. The pastor had preached a sermon and gave an altar call for various needs. He had called for people who needed healing to come forward, and he prayed for them. As they returned to their seats, he called for anyone praying for the spiritual gift of speaking in tongues to come to the altar. That invitation caught my attention.

A year before, sometime after my conversion experience, my coworker and friend Cosette said, "I've been praying for you. You haven't received everything; there is more." I knew she was talking about evidence of being filled with the Holy Spirit. I didn't respond to her, but I had been praying about receiving the gift of speaking in tongues.

At the worship service, I turned to my friend Emily and asked, "Did he say speaking in tongues?" She said, "Yes."

Launching into the Unknown

I got up and went to the altar for prayer.

The pastor prayed and laid hands on each person at the altar, and then he said, "Speak, speak."

With my hands raised, I tried to speak, but nothing happened.

He said again, "Speak, speak," as his hand touched my forehead. I returned to my seat thinking this was not my time to receive God's gift.

About three months later, I phoned an elderly woman from the West Indies, Mrs. Murray, who attended our church and told her what had happened in the Bahamas. I knew that she spoke in tongues. This gift was not practiced in our church body.

I said, "What do I need to do? I know speaking in tongues is a gift God wants to give me."

She said, "Baby, you have to tarry."

"What does that mean?"

"Get on your knees and pray. Place your hand on your stomach and rub upward. Just trust the Lord."

I followed her instructions that evening. I don't recall how long I waited, maybe an hour. Then, I started speaking in tongues, an unknown language. I sang in tongues also. Later, speaking in tongues would become a part of my prayer life as I communed with God and replenished my soul. Rausch discusses times when we recognize God's presence, and speaking in tongues is one of several spiritual gifts listed in 1 Cor 12. He says, "The charismata or spiritual gifts are a manifestation of the Spirit's presence."[5] I received what God had told my spirit he would give me, but it was in his timing and manner, and I was home alone. He was equipping me for service.

On another occasion, God spoke to me in a Sunday morning worship service. Dr. Sampson preached a sermon from Eph 3:13, "I ask you, therefore, not to be discouraged because of my sufferings for you, which are your glory," and Acts 20:22, "And now, compelled by the Spirit, I am going to Jerusalem, not knowing what will happen to me there." My pastor said, "God will not lead you where *you* want to go, but if you choose to go where he leads you, he will never leave you. You'll find joy once you come into the consciousness of your purpose."

This was it! "You'll find joy once you come into the consciousness of your purpose." I now realize this was a crucial part of what had been missing in my life. It was connected to what triggered me to recognize

---

5. Rausch, *Ignatian Retreat*, 19.

something was missing when I walked off the dance floor at happy hour, several months before my conversion. It was connected to being set apart for service and going where the Spirit led me. I would never experience true joy if I continued to sail along doing my will instead of yielding to God's will. Or if I kept looking for love in all the wrong places. Sin prevents us from recognizing our purpose in life.

Dr. Sampson cautioned us in his sermon: "Don't try to move out of an experience too soon. If you do, you may not learn all that the Lord wants you to know. If you fix your eyes on God, he will move you into the authenticity of your personhood. He'll change your name and change your destiny. Your personality will be greater than your history."

It would happen a few years later that I tried to move too quickly from a situation, but God was there to teach me.

When Dr. Sampson preached, it was about what he had experienced himself. I, too, wanted to find that joy and go through whatever God had planned for me.

Now I understand that God began melting and molding me to love him with all my heart, soul, mind, and strength. He put this desire in me, and it grew stronger and stronger. My lifetime Scriptures were Matt 6:33 (KJV), "Seek ye first the kingdom of God . . . and all these things shall be added unto you," and Isa 64:8 (KJV), "But now, O Lord, thou art our father; we are the clay, and thou our potter; and we all are the work of thy hand." God was setting me apart to live for him and not the world.

Knowing God, I would find my identity, who he says I am. Loving God, I would learn to trust him in all things. I knew that God had begun a good work in me, and he would carry it through. Serving God, I would use whatever he gives me to share with others.

Now I realize that losing my job in marketing was the launchpad into the uncharted waters of being unemployed. God had led me to "the place where another layer of transformation occurs, and a renewed life of faith begins for those who feel called and have the courage to move into it."[6] As a result of being in this place, it was inevitable that my spiritual journey would take me to unfamiliar places and new experiences. It would be a time of letting go and letting God align my will with his will.

On my spiritual journey, God would remove the barriers that prevented me from being the beloved woman he created me to be and teach me his ways, a lifetime process.

---

6. Hagberg and Guelich, *Critical Journey*, 114.

Above all things, I would not be alone. God had his hand on me, molding and shaping me in his image.

STONE OF REMEMBRANCE: SANCTIFICATION

In Greek, sanctification means "to make holy." God sanctifies us. Our role is to purify ourselves from everything that contaminates body and spirit, perfecting holiness out of reverence for God (2 Cor 7:1). I was learning to live in obedience to God through his word and the Spirit's leading. I was being set apart for God's will.

REFLECTION QUESTIONS

Thinking back, can you name a specific incident in your life when it required an act of faith in life or your calling? What did you learn that kept you on course? Was there someone or something meaningful that helped along the way? In what ways did God come through in an unexpected way? What is your stone of remembrance?

6

Waiting for the Peach Cobbler

> Waiting for the Lord is not passive it is active.
> We're waiting for God's intervention.
> It is wise to wait because he gives us clear direction. . . . We wait until he is ready to give it. . . . We are walking in step with God, not the world.
> —Charles Stanley

THERE WERE NO INDICATIONS that I would have any problem waiting on God to lead me into the next chapter in my life. He would direct my path with clear signposts. In the meantime, as I thought about what was next, from my large living room window, I saw a coworker from my previous employment walking briskly through my neighborhood one morning. He looked good and healthy, although I knew he had a mental health concern. It had been over a year since he left work. I wondered how he was doing, if he would ever work again. Then I thought, "What about me? Will I ever work again?" Although I was hopeful, to be honest, the thought came to mind. I know what it's like to feel or think God has forgotten me.

My friends faithfully prayed for me. I reminded them to pray for God's will, not necessarily a job. I knew God brought me out of the corporate environment for a good reason, and I wanted to know why.

I figured the church would be a good place to go during the week because there was always something to get involved with, like the times I ate with the underprivileged people during our lunch meals in the fellowship hall downstairs. As my eyes surveyed the room, I wondered what their story was. Although I did not linger on their circumstances, I could not forget the looks on their faces; there was no sense of time or a need to do anything else but enjoy and stay in the moment. They likely didn't have jobs, and I perceived some of them were homeless. I thought, "Could that be me one day? I couldn't imagine it could be, but could it? What will be my story after I make it through the unknown?"

In the morning after I was up for a while, I said, "Lord, I am available to you as I wait." I know that sounds risky, but I was willing to be curious and open to the Spirit. I went to our church again. That day, I washed chairs on the lower level with a retired couple, the Crenshaws. It took three hours, but oh, what fellowship. The Crenshaws were short-term missionaries in the United States. They were ordinary people with big hearts. Mrs. Crenshaw was an outgoing woman who taught Vacation Bible School and children's songs. She introduced me to the eighteenth-century hymn "Let All the People Praise Thee," recapturing our glorious God and what he has done for us. I was blessed when she read Ps 67, which became one of my favorite psalms:

> May God be gracious to us and bless us
> and make his face shine on us—
> so that your ways may be known on earth,
> your salvation among all nations.
>
> May the peoples praise you, God;
> may all the peoples praise you.
> May the nations be glad and sing for joy,
> for you rule the peoples with equity
> and guide the nations of the earth.
> (Ps 67: 1–4)

The Crenshaws loved the Lord and served others for kingdom purposes. Psalm 90:17 mirrors their lives and their effect on others: "And let the beauty of the LORD our God be upon us, and establish the work of our hands for us; yes, establish the work of our hands." They didn't mind getting their hands wet, cooking to feed our neighbors, and being in the spotlight. They wanted to use everything God had given them to serve until the Lord called them home. They gave me a pin that emphasized their passion for serving. It says, "God's retirement is out of this world." I never wore it on my jacket, but it remained on my nightstand for years as a reminder of a kingdom principle. I remembered this principle and passed it along to others.

Although I wasn't working in a regular job, I was active and growing, and I stayed connected to my church community. One day, I stopped by my church and saw Dr. Sampson in the hallway.

"I'm still waiting on the Lord," I said. I thought he would be pleased to get a status report.

"God will give you the peach cobbler when you least expect it."

I laughed because I like peach cobbler. I'd not heard this expression. I loved it. Peach cobbler is a traditional African American favorite, especially during the holidays. It would be worth waiting for God to give me my peach cobbler. Pastor Sampson always gave words of encouragement. I could almost taste and see the peach cobbler.

Driving home, I thought about the blessings of being loved and cared for. I had the support of my family and friends as I went through uncharted waters. They genuinely wanted to know how I was doing. I was able to manage well. When I could not pay my few bills on time, I placed them on my dining room table, laid my hands on them, and prayed for wisdom to know when and which to pay. Fortunately, I did not lie awake at night thinking about whether I'd be able to pay my bills. I prayed to the Lord, trusting he would work things out for my good. I was always in a sweet spot when I received meal dates, gifts of money, or "just because" notes in a lovely bouquet of flowers.

Things were good because I made do with what I had. When the bumper on my 1984 Nissan Maxima detached slightly, I did not incur an unnecessary repair bill. Instead, I drove carefully to avoid hitting potholes, keeping the bumper in place. One fiercely chilly winter morning, I pulled into the church parking lot. It was less than half full because many cars wouldn't start. I was grateful that my old "Betsy" started right up.

I felt different when my cousin Cheryl visited me from Alabama for my birthday. We attended an afternoon Sunday service, at which Dr. Sampson was preaching. When the service was over, we went to the parking lot and got in the car to leave. Old Betsy wouldn't start, and it wasn't cold outside. I was at a tipping point. I cried and complained about my car. I had always had a new vehicle, but not now. I was upset and pitiful on my birthday. Being upset rarely happens to me. I imagined myself saying, "What do you want from me, Lord? Please tell me."

Cheryl had been on this journey into the unknown with me from the beginning. My friends, Doris Stanley and Reverend Spruill, and Cheryl came to my aid. A new battery was purchased and exchanged for the old battery. I calmed down when I heard the car start. The car's purr was a wonderful birthday gift. Afterwards, I thought, "Why didn't I just trust God?"

I was in the Lord's school of learning. I was learning to have childlike faith without a safety net as I navigated the unknown. I was sometimes unable to help myself, but God used others when I couldn't. With each challenge, I kept looking back at what he had done already to help me remain encouraged.

While in the church office one day, I got excited when I saw an invitation to attend a Pastors' Fellowship Breakfast and an evening rally in Detroit at a local church. Dr. Tony Evans, pastor of Oak Cliff Bible Fellowship and president of The Urban Alternative, would be the guest speaker. I had listened to Dr. Evans regularly for a couple of years.

One of the staff pastors, Rev. Lemuel Harrison, said, "Here's something you might want to check out."

I said, "All right! Yes. I will. Thank you." God was watching out for me. I'd listened to Dr. Evans many times on the radio.

"Do you think you'll go?"

"Oh, yes. I'll call and register today." I smiled. He'd heard me talk about The Urban Alternative in the past. I was going to attend as a representative of Tabernacle Church.

I called to register. My name was placed on the list, and I was told someone would give me a call soon.

Well, I waited for days, then three weeks had gone by. No call. I called again. This time, my call was transferred to the pastor. I was disappointed to learn that my gender was an issue. I was a woman! I couldn't let it go. I wondered if the host church had thought I wouldn't call if I did not hear from someone.

A week before the prayer breakfast, I received a call from my friend and spiritual companion, Bill. He asked if I would be willing to go to the Detroit Metro Airport to pick up Mrs. Lois Evans, Dr. Evans's wife, and take her to the hotel where they were staying. I hadn't known that Bill was on the event planning committee. I was surprised that he'd asked me. I didn't have a prestigious title, high status in the community, or a luxury car. I did have a good running car, and I enjoyed meeting new people. I felt overjoyed for days to serve in this capacity.

I recognized Mrs. Evans at the luggage carousel when I entered Detroit Metro Airport. I held up a sign with her name on it. Mrs. Evans's beauty radiated. After putting her luggage in the trunk of old "Betsy," with over two hundred thousand miles on it, we began our fifty-minute drive to her hotel to meet Dr. Evans.

I was surprised when she asked me what was happening in my life. I started by briefly describing my corporate unemployment experience, but then I had to tell her what was on my heart. So, I seized the moment and told her about the Pastors' Fellowship Breakfast dilemma and the pastor of the host church telling me I could not come because I was a woman.

I liked the way Mrs. Evans responded. She made no promises but was willing to bring this matter to Dr. Evans's attention. She was concerned; she cared about me. My burden had lightened, and I was hopeful about joining the Detroit pastors and Dr. Tony Evans at the breakfast table.

After we had arrived at the hotel, I hurried to get her luggage out of the trunk. I was honored to serve her. She promised to talk to Dr. Evans about my situation after his radio interview. She said she would call me back.

As soon as she entered the hotel lobby, I left, praising God for this divine appointment. About two hours later, Lois Evans called, as she said she would, with the message, "Dr. Evans would love for you to join us." This was my signpost from God. He is the Master of everything.

At the breakfast, I confidently walked into the room as a woman given grace and favor. Mrs. Evans saw me coming. Our eyes connected. She sat at the front table with her husband, surrounded by about twenty-five pastors. I saw an elderly gentleman close to the door where I came in; he invited me to take the empty seat next to him. We chatted briefly. With a smile of welcome, he asked if I were a pastor or minister. I said, "No, I've listened to Dr. Evans on the radio and wanted to hear what he has to say regarding our churches."

Dr. Evans welcomed us and prayed. I was happy and encouraged about being there. I hadn't known what God was doing behind the scenes to make a way for me to attend, but he taught me that he is not limited by our theological, biblical, or human barriers. He is God, and he opens and closes doors. Since this experience, I have not attempted to force the opening or closing of doors. I let God be the navigator. Later, I would face similar barriers in places where I was a minority, but I had learned to see the hand of the Lord at work for his good.

A week later, I called Bill to thank him for the opportunity to meet the Evanses. I also wanted to know about any Bible studies besides our church's.

He said, "Yep, I know one. There's a daytime Bible study taught by Brother Owen Fraser at a senior citizens apartment complex." Bill was always resourceful. The Bible study was less than two miles from my house.

I said, "Oh, Brother Fraser." I had heard his name many times from my father. My father had taken classes taught by him. He was an adjunct teacher at Detroit Bible College, later known as William Tyndale College. "He's got a great reputation for teaching God's word."

He laughed. "He was the man you sat beside at the pastors' breakfast."

"Wow. We didn't have a chance to introduce ourselves. He asked me if I was a pastor or minister."

In the evening, I phoned Brother Fraser. He welcomed me to the ecumenical Bible study. I had the pleasure of sitting at the table with a middle-aged woman confined to a wheelchair and three women in their eighties. I heard many stories of God's faithfulness. One of the founders of Detroit's United Conference of Women (UCW), the most prominent African American Christian women's conference in the eighties and nineties, was the most senior woman in the Bible study. The UCW began in 1976, and each year its participation tripled. It is still growing strong in equipping the next generation of African American women today.

By the time I arrived at our Bible study meetings, this broad shouldered, stern senior was settled in her wheelchair at the head of the table. She was the embodiment of the strength, commitment, and spirit of the black woman equipping other women. She was a trailblazer. I imagined how she felt knowing her work was not in vain. It's satisfying to know when we've kept the faith until the end.

After two years of Bible study, it was time for this part of my journey to end and for me to begin new ministry opportunities. Brother Fraser, although he was a member of the same denomination as the host church for the pastors' breakfast, affirmed my calling and blessed me, along with the women, as I continued to follow Christ. I was blessed to be in the presence of committed people who were still bearing fruit. These are the people God put in my path to shape me.

I continued being available to God for service. He closes one door and opens another. I won't forget the invitation I received for my first trip to the Bahamas. After Sunday morning worship, Brenda Hague, the ministry coordinator, asked me to be part of a delegation to go to Nassau, the Bahamas, and one of the seven Family Islands. I was available but couldn't afford to use my savings for nonessential purposes. Brenda had arranged for me to receive a loan from an undisclosed lender until I could pay it back in full.

Then I realized I didn't have the appropriate clothes. I called my cousin Cheryl after she returned to Alabama. I casually mentioned my trip to the Bahamas and laughed about not having anything to wear.

I said, "I wasn't thinking, I don't have anything appropriate to wear."

"Oh, that's no problem. I'll let Pam know, and she'll hook you up. Don't worry about that. We've got it. You know my sister loves to shop."

"Wow! That would be wonderful. Let me know."

I couldn't believe it. Pam knew precisely what I needed to be comfortable in hot weather. She was a pro shopper. United Parcel Service dropped off an oversized box from Alabama within two weeks. Pam sent loose-fitting cotton dresses, flare and pencil skirts, and short-sleeved tops, all in my favorite bright colors. I received more than I could imagine, and I loved everything because they fit well. I had enough clothes to accommodate all three of my trips to the Bahamas. Romans 8:28 is enlightening. It says, "And we know that in all things God works for the good of those who love him, who have been called according to his purpose."

On the Nassau juncture of my first trip to the Bahamas, our bus passed by the downtown marketplace on the way to our hotel. I saw a man with dark-colored pants and a white shirt with a Bible in his hand standing at a podium with several folding chairs. A few people stood on the sidelines. I looked forward to checking into the hotel and returning downtown to satisfy my curiosity about what they were trying to accomplish.

I returned alone to the marketplace downtown and learned that a local group was hosting a Bible Marathon, a twenty-four-hour nonstop reading from Genesis to Revelation. It was located on Bay Street, only five blocks from the hotel. The location and weather were perfect. I took a seat in the front. A person could sit and listen or be invited to the podium to read from the Bible. I had never heard of or participated in a Bible Marathon indoors or outdoors.

God's word is living, active, and sharper than any double-edged sword. The group leaders and participants didn't know whose hearts and ears were open to receive, but God's word would accomplish what he pleased.

A young lady came over and asked me if I wanted to read. With enthusiasm, I went to the podium three times in two days to read aloud from Job 42, Pss 1–4 and 27, Amos, Nahum, and Isaiah. Several passages related to my spiritual journey at the time. The words came alive and meant something to me then, especially Job 42:2: "I know that you can do all things; no purpose of yours can be thwarted." I was reminded yet again to trust God's guidance and faithfulness.

Two or three days later, the front desk hotel manager called me to come to the lobby. I was greeted by two of the Bible Marathon elders. They told me how long it had taken them to finish reading the Bible. It was a joyous moment, and I was glad to have taken part in reading the whole Bible in the public square with people I had never met, but the word of God brought us together.

There were other times when the word of God brought people together. At our Saturday night Bible study at Tabernacle Baptist Church, in addition to the Bible study, our octogenarian assistant pastor, Rev. Gordon Story, welcomed testimonies of what God had done in our lives. Testimonies are remembering God and what he has done and sharing it with others. A designated time set aside for testimonies is prevalent in the black church.

In a circle of about fifteen people, I enthusiastically shared how God had taken care of me over the last year when I was unemployed. I said, "I don't know if God will lead me to live outside of Michigan, go overseas, or stay in Detroit, but I trust that he is leading me somewhere."

At the end of our time together, Reverend Story's eyes scanned the circle with a look I'd seen before. I accepted his invitation to close our time with prayer. Within a few seconds, a small, friendly child accompanied by an adult I'd never seen before walked up to me. Before my conversion, and as an adult, babies and toddlers didn't usually respond favorably toward me. I stooped, reached out to pick him up, and began praying. He showed no fear as his little arms wrapped around my neck.

In the prayer, I praised God for his faithfulness and provisions for us that week. I thanked him for Reverend Story's faithful service, the night's lesson, and our safety while traveling home. I asked God to bring us back to church tomorrow to worship him. We all hugged and left the church.

That night at home, God met me in a prayer of praise and thanksgiving for our Spirit-led Saturday gathering; I wrote in my journal, "God will hold my hand *and will enlarge my footsteps so my feet will not slip.* God will show me what he wants me to pray for and who to lay hands on. He will work through me to draw people to himself. He has forgiven me for all my sins." These words were hidden in my heart, then and now. I wanted to be attentive to God's presence and reach out to him instead of trying to do things alone.

God calls us to be like children. In the Gospel, Jesus tells his disciples in Matt 18:3 that they will never enter the kingdom of heaven unless they "become like children." I cherished the image of a child and our awesome God with outstretched hands, inviting us to come and trust him. His hands can be gentle, firm, and strong. God met me through a child's trust in me. He would be there for me and carry me through life's challenges, even in this time of uncertainty. I knew it would be critical for me to trust and obey. The powerful image of God *enlarging my footsteps so my feet would not slip* is as relevant today as it was then.

I often recall the image of my feet not slipping when I must focus on God instead of my circumstances. It is a practice I learned to anchor my soul. The Holy Spirit draws my attention to what God says he will do versus what I think I should do. When I allow him to lead, I know where I stand and can trust him for my path forward in his timing. My feet are firm. This thinking contradicts my way of living before my conversion. I am learning God's ways and promises, as in Prov 3:5–6: "Trust in the Lord with all your heart, and lean not on your own understanding. In all your ways, submit to him, and he will make your paths straight."

Late in the summer of 1992, I visited my paternal uncle and aunt at their home in Florence, Alabama. He and his wife lived quietly but were regularly involved in the church. My uncle was a retired African Methodist Episcopal (AME) Church pastor but was now legally blind. I always enjoyed my visits with Uncle Obie and his wife, Juanita. She had instilled in me the beauty of traveling, seeing beyond my backyard, by telling me about her enjoyment of traveling to various places on behalf of their denomination, and she had given me a small piece of travel luggage when I graduated high school.

That summer visit was the most memorable of all. As my uncle and I sat at the kitchen table while my aunt prepared a meal, I casually asked him, "What is a favorite psalm of yours?"

As he leaned back in his red plaid shirt and black dress pants held up by suspenders, wearing thick, round glasses and a broad smile, he said, "Psalm 18." His King James Version of the Bible was nearby on a bookcase, so I reached for it and held his giant print Bible in my hands. I felt honored to read God's word to him. I began reading all fifty verses. The following verses caught my attention:

I will love thee, O Lord, my strength....
He maketh my feet like hinds' feet, and setteth me upon my high places.
He teacheth my hands to war, so that a bow of steel is broken by mine arms.
Thou hast also given me the shield of thy salvation: and thy right hand hath holden me up, and thy gentleness hath made me great.
Thou hast enlarged my steps under me, that my feet did not slip.
(Ps 18:1, 33–36 KJV)

God met me through the same message, with the image of enlarging my footsteps as I had journaled and later read in Ps 18 to my uncle. I pictured God's activity in King David's life in this psalm. David's feet were secure, and he was intentionally exalted in high places. His feet would not slip from under him. His hands were prepared for physical and spiritual warfare. David stood confidently, as God's hand held him up.

As I read Ps 18, "I will love thee, O Lord, my strength," at times, Reverend Posie slightly tilted his head and smiled. He had fought for his country in the US Army in World War II and courageously lived through Jim Crow laws and segregation in the South. He bravely endured failing health. His feet did not slip because he trusted in God. Yes, I was encouraged by my uncle's Christian witness. Reverend Posie was secure, solid, and unwavering in his faith. This kind of faith didn't just happen. God had brought him through the storms in life, including his health.

God taught me to love and trust him through my pastor, church, family, friends, relatives, strangers, and community by how he used them to encourage and support me. I knew God's hand would hold me up also. Change was coming soon. I didn't expect what happened next.

One day, I sat quietly in my favorite chair in the living room, sipping coffee and watching TV. The phone rang. I recognized the company name by the caller ID. It was the first sign of hope. I'd been waiting for a breakthrough.

A significant computer software company asked about my interest in a contractual position with a state government agency. It seemed like a good fit because I would interact with a population beyond the four walls of the agency. I received an appointment for an interview and felt encouraged. A week before the interview, I received a call from the company indicating the contract had fallen through.

I felt let down, and I asked God what he wanted me to do. I didn't get a response. I was ready to have some structure and purpose for getting up every morning.

A few days later, I was contacted to take an examination for an upper-level position in a revenue office in Detroit; however, I ranked number four. I also thought that would have been a good fit in terms of salary, benefits, and location, but it was not where God was calling me. I felt let down again.

I was reminded of what God told me earlier about my feet not slipping in Ps 18. I reread it, reflected on it, and journaled my thoughts. I believed in God, but waiting for another sign of hope had become a struggle. I held on though.

I knew people with influence and the ability to connect me to potential work leads, but I got none. I actively read the employment ads in the local paper and sent many personalized cover letters with resumes printed on fine linen paper. I had a stack of canned rejection letters on my dining room table, but I kept trying.

Eventually, I felt like the rivers had dried up. It was senseless to keep fishing if nothing was biting. Apparently, God had something for me. I had asked my home Bible study friends to pray that God's will be done. I knew he had a plan for me, but I didn't know what it was. He was preparing me for something for which I wasn't ready. It would come in God's timing; at least, this is what I kept telling myself.

My unemployment created a deep hole in my life. Some of the things that were taken away from me had played a crucial role in a fulfilling work experience—status, presence, usefulness, being part of a team with purpose-driven goals, and a good, steady paycheck.

One afternoon, after getting out of my car to enter the church, a fellow member and minister's wife, Marsha, came out of the church door. She was a seasoned schoolteacher who loved her job. She said to me, "The Detroit Public Schools is hiring substitute teachers. I think you'd better check it out."

"All right, thank you. I'll call the main office tomorrow." I was trying to be polite, but I did not want to make that call. Nevertheless, I had an inner conviction to follow this lead. Before making the call, I knew this was where God wanted me, although it wasn't my choice. I had always said, "You could not pay me enough to teach in a school." If God wanted me in the classroom, that's where I would go.

I was hired immediately, and the two and a half years of teaching primarily third graders were grueling. In Vacation Bible School in church, I always taught the middle schoolers. Other than an orientation, there was little preparation for taking on responsibilities of this magnitude in a classroom, although I came with some transferable skills. This was a Jonah experience; I didn't want to go, but I went out of obedience. I remembered what Dr. Sampson had said: "If you choose to go where he leads you, he will never leave you."

I was quickly given Emergency Substitute in a Regular Position (ESRP) status, which meant I was assigned to one school for an entire year or longer in the same classroom and received more pay and some benefits. I felt trapped, and even with the increase, I was underpaid. I worked at three schools in this position. Each school differed, and my purpose for working at each was unique.

No one knew about the blessings that came with praying for each student as I greeted them at the classroom door or when I learned of their challenges at home and in their neighborhoods. Some students had adult-sized responsibilities imposed on them.

One teacher noticed the popular NIV *Women's Devotional Bible*, which had recently been published, on my desk. The news about where to find a Bible spread quickly. I sold ten Bibles at that school. An expert teacher became a friend and member of Tabernacle Missionary Baptist Church through an invitation to visit our church. I was reminded that God was everywhere in the world, working his redemptive plan. I prayed for administrators, teachers, and staff.

Still, I wanted more than teaching, and I thought perhaps God was calling me to become a principal if I stayed in the public schools, which would align better with my experience, gifts, and interests. I started part-time classes toward that end at the University of Detroit Mercy. I did well in all classes and enjoyed them. One of my professors asked me to come to his district after I finished the MA in the special education program. I earned credits equivalent to one full-time year. I did not know it then, but God wasn't calling me to work in education. It seemed the right direction if I would have remained in this field, but God was navigating my journey. I was learning how to discern his will and hear his voice. There were still more lessons for me to learn.

At times, I felt helpless because there wasn't a natural fit in education for me. I was not fulfilled as a teacher, but God was developing my character, particularly patience. I learned to be resilient and courageous. During the evenings and weekends, I attended Bible studies, worship services, and Christian training events with my friends to fill my cup.

During this same time, I had a few dreams. Each time I woke up, I knew I had been preaching in my sleep in a multiracial environment. When I mentioned my experience to a senior minister in the church community, he said, "Don't think God isn't going to do something in your life to satisfy the desire he has given you. Your dreams are your mission." I believed that if God had given me something to do, he would make his will known to me.

Through a series of events and convictions, I yearned to receive biblical training at a deeper level. I was familiar with the graduate schools in Michigan; however, I wanted to go out of state. I went to my local library to research seminaries in the Midwest and Southeast. I made a list of eleven schools. I contacted them and then narrowed my list to three. I couldn't visit all three, so I chose to visit Columbia International University's (CIU) graduate school in South Carolina because of its focus on global mission and practical biblical theology.

I took a plane to Nashville, Tennessee, and my cousin Cheryl and I drove to Columbia. We had a wonderful time together. Dr. Sampson had given me the names of three local churches and pastors he knew and one administrative person at the seminary. He had preached revivals at Brookland, Ridgewood, and Haskell Heights Baptist churches annually. Cheryl and I visited Ridgewood Baptist's evening Bible study the moment we arrived in Columbia. They were glad we came.

The next day, when we saw the Monticello Road exit off Interstate 20 East, we got excited. Within ten minutes we were at the entrance of CIU. We took the long drive onto the campus. Cheryl said, and I felt, "This is where you belong." From that moment, we sensed God's presence. We tried not to be too excited. The conversations with admissions and current graduate students, a campus tour, and an opportunity to sit in a theology class felt right.

It also felt right to have an unscheduled opportunity to chat with the only African American faculty member, Dr. Charles Young. I had intended to make an appointment with him ahead of time, but with all the preparation for the trip, I had forgotten. We happened to meet in the hallway at 8:15 a.m., and he invited us into his office for a conversation. I was convinced that I belonged here. I felt like I was about to begin my second half of life at CIU.

Waiting for the Peach Cobbler

Early in the year, I heard a well-known radio pastor, Chuck Swindoll, talk about knowing God's voice when he wants you to move. He said you can know it when

1. there's uneasiness in your present situation;
2. you are willing to move, give up your home, and move to unfamiliar territory;
3. the message from people, through sermons and conversations, won't go away; and
4. you see a pattern to where God is leading you.

I had experienced each one of the points in his sermon. I was convinced that God was speaking to me. Making the move seemed right, and I was ready to sell my house and go to seminary to prepare for full-time ministry. There was nothing else I wanted to do more. Although I didn't know it at that time, I wasn't done waiting for the peach cobbler.

STONE OF REMEMBRANCE: GUIDANCE

During a long wait for my next assignment after being unemployed for a time, I was encouraged when I remembered God's word that he would enlarge my footsteps so my feet would not slip. He guided my steps in his word, through individuals and the Spirit, as I waited on him. God makes our paths straight, even when it doesn't seem like it (Prov 3:6).

REFLECTION QUESTIONS

Are there any God encounters when you had to wait a long time to move forward in ministry or life? If so, describe what God was working in your life as you waited. What gave you peace or unrest? What is your stone of remembrance?

7

Oh, Taste and See!

May all that you bring to the world through your writing and living shine forth to help rebuild the heart of the world. —A friend

Each day I tried to start my day with hope, trusting that I was living within God's will. When I was at home one day, the phone rang, and I hurried to answer it. It was the admissions office at CIU. I had been accepted into the MDiv program for the intercultural studies track, starting in the fall. After getting off the phone, I danced and cried, "Yes!" A few days later, I found a letter from the seminary on the table requesting a deposit for tuition, room, and board. I felt good, knowing I would put a check in the mail the next day, and I breathed a sigh of relief. I thought, "I'm on my way." I had been waiting for the peach cobbler. I felt peaceful, excited, and emotionally ready to get the ball rolling to move to Columbia, South Carolina.

Several weeks after I had shared my fantastic news with my family, friends, and some of my church family, I arrived at the church for the eleven o'clock Sunday service. I came through the back door, which leads to the sanctuary on the left and a hallway to the conference room on the right. The ministers, trustees, and deacons were in their clergy robes and black suits, headed into the conference room for prayer. I saw the assistant pastor, Reverend Story, as I approached the main floor. His eyes landed on me, and he asked if I would join him in the conference room. I was honored to be in the room during prayer time before the service for the first time. I joined the men and one or two women officers in a large circle. Reverend Story turned to me and asked me to give the prayer.

Deacon McCutcheon said, "Tell everyone why you're asking her to pray."

Reverend Story said, "She'll be going to seminary in September. She'll be leaving us to move to Columbia, South Carolina."

The clergy and officers smiled and belted out, "Praise the Lord!" "Congratulations!" They clapped. I was grateful, and then I shifted their attention to what mattered by saying, "Let us pray." Then, I prayed.

There would be time for questions and sharing my plans later. In another meeting, one of the deacons said, "Don't stay away too long. We want you to return to Detroit about two or three times a year." I was grateful for the love and support my church showed me.

I felt like God was preparing the way for me, but I also felt overwhelmed by everything I needed to do before moving to Columbia. I began painting the living room, dining room, and bedrooms, throwing things out, and making everything presentable to make a good impression on prospective buyers. I contacted the realtor a friend recommended, and my house went on the market.

As I continued to get things ready for the move to Columbia, I started having some doubts about the sale of my house. Something seemed wrong. Instead of the ball rolling along, it seemed like I was facing a ball of confusion. I knew that "God is not the author of confusion, but of peace" (1 Cor 14:33 KJV), so this made me wonder. At one point, a friend offered me a shortcut by trying to connect me with a city inspector she knew. She said she would act as the middle person. Instead of making things go smoothly, this turned out to complicate things because we hadn't gone through the main office of the City of Detroit. I finally put an end to this attempt by contacting the city myself. After that, the process went well from beginning to end. The city inspection was completed, and I took care of a few violations.

After that, a single woman made an offer, but I needed to decline it. Then a young couple was interested, but they didn't follow through to make a bid. A gentleman made an offer by late summer, but his credit fell through. Several other people expressed an interest informally, but nothing materialized. It was a disappointing time for me.

I wondered what God was saying to me. Had I misread what the well-known radio pastor said about knowing God's voice when he wants you to move? I shared my feelings of uneasiness with Dr. Sampson before one of our church meetings.

I said, "I think God is trying to tell me something."

He said, "What makes you say that?"

"I've had three potential buyers, but those didn't work out. Several other people expressed an interest, but nothing came through."

"What is your main concern?"

"I won't be able to start school in the fall if I don't sell my house, although I've been thinking about going to seminary and letting the realtor handle it while I'm there."

Dr. Sampson said, "God's delay is not his denial."

"So, in other words, my timing might not be his timing?"

"Yes. That's right."

"Oh." I thought about this carefully. Because of what Dr. Sampson said, I realized I didn't know *when* I was supposed to go to seminary. I only knew I was *supposed* to go. As much as I didn't want to believe it, what Dr. Sampson said made sense to me. I recalled him saying previously, "Don't try to move out of an experience too soon. If you do, you may not learn all that the Lord wants you to know."

Dr. Sampson hugged me, and before walking away, he said, "Just remember you have a friend; you'll always have a friend."

At the time, I also understood this to mean what the songwriter describes in "What a Friend We Have in Jesus." We have "a friend so faithful." He is always there to hear and respond to our prayers. Now I know that sometimes God doesn't tell us everything about what he wants us to do at once. He leads one step at a time. I began to accept that I had to wait until God told me when. God has taught me through this experience and others to listen deeply. I had assumed it was *right now* when he told me to go to seminary. Really, it wasn't. I'm a "git 'er done" kind of person, but more learning, knowing, and experiencing God lay ahead.

When I thought about Dr. Sampson's words, I realized maybe I wasn't really done yet with waiting for the peach cobbler. Three days after that conversation, I took my house off the market. I understood much later that there were things God had wanted to accomplish in me before I went to Columbia. Isaiah 40:31 has become a favorite of mine: "But they that wait upon the LORD shall renew their strength; they shall mount up with wings as eagles; they shall run, and not be weary; and they shall walk, and not faint." I waited.

Stage three, "The Productive Life," of *The Critical Journey* rings true to where I was in my spiritual journey. "Having been given to and having received so much from our association with others, the time of reciprocity has come. It is now our turn to give in return."[1]

Several days after taking my house off the market, I received a phone call that someone I'd known when I was growing up was in the hospital. The news about John was not good. He was not expected to live. When I contacted his mother, she asked me to visit John. This took quite a shift for me, since I'd been focusing on my move. I had not seen any of John's family members for years. I had visited the sick in the past but not anyone outside of my own family who was expected to die soon.

When I walked into John's hospital room, I somberly greeted his mother, father, grandmother, and sister. Then I greeted John. His head leaned into his chest, and he whispered, "Hi, Denise. Thank you for coming." He didn't make sounds of being in pain. My spoken response was brief, as I expressed God's presence and assurance. Then I invited everyone to join hands for prayer.

After acknowledging God as our Heavenly Father and reminding us of his great love and promise to be with John until the end, I said, "Lord, I ask for your forgiveness of John's sins, and for the sins of anyone else who needs your forgiveness. May this family take this opportunity to forgive each other. Help them to stick together during this difficult time."

After the prayer, I ended with words of comfort and said goodbye. John's mother asked to walk with me downstairs. As we walked, I wondered what had prompted me to give John and his family an opportunity to forgive each other. At the same time, I felt God extending his love, grace, and mercy to them in their midnight hour.

In the lobby, I asked John's mother, "Have there been family problems or concerns?" She implied that there had been emotional abuse, and she had been wounded by harsh words. I knew very little about their family relationships. The grandmother and sister came to the lobby and sat in an area distant from us, leaving John and his father alone. Then John's mother shared a family secret and said, "I want peace about this situation."

I asked her to confess and ask God's forgiveness for anything she may have done concerning it. She agreed to pray with me. Then, I gave some words of comfort and offered my assistance later if needed. She cried.

---

1. Hagberg and Guelich, *Critical Journey*, 73.

As I said my goodbyes, Mrs. Lewis said, "I noticed something different about you when you came into John's room."

I told her, "I'll be leaving soon to go to seminary in Columbia, South Carolina, to study to become a minister of God's word." We hugged again. "I'll continue to pray for John and your family," I said.

I left the hospital thanking God for his presence and grace. Then, I went to the nursing home for my regular weekly visit to my Uncle Jake. I always ended up visiting other patients in their rooms or in the hallways. It appeared dark as I walked past patients and staff in the long hallway, and I saw sickness, frailty, and blank faces. Patients were holding onto railings on the walls, sitting in wheelchairs, or shuffling along.

Yet, I also saw light shining through the darkness: I saw nurses and staff attending to residents' needs, visitors coming to see their loved ones. A man in his wheelchair at the entrance sang his favorite songs. I had no doubt that God was there. After spending time catching up with Uncle Jake and gathering his laundry to take home, I walked into the room of a patient who couldn't get out of her oversized bed, not easily even with assistance. I'd visited her before. She didn't speak, but she smiled when I softly sang "Blessed Assurance" and prayed with her.

When I got home, I thought through my day and realized I was spent. Later that evening, I got a call that John had passed. I was sad but grateful for being there with him and his family in his last moments in this life.

I was grateful I could minister to John and his family, but I was also curious about my prayer regarding family matters. One evening when I arrived early at church for the Sunday school teachers' meeting to prepare for the upcoming lesson, I saw Deacon Brown, a Sunday school teacher. He was knowledgeable about the Bible and spiritual practices, and he didn't mind sharing.

I told Deacon Brown about my prayer with John's family and that I had prayed with them about dealing with any unfinished family matters. I said, "Deacon Brown, sometimes I know things about people that were revealed to me that I could not have known on my own. In this case, I didn't know if I was being judgmental or if the Holy Spirit had shown me that something was needed. I've read about discernment, but I don't understand it practically."

I had read in *The Gifts of the Spirit* that discernment is based on 1 Cor 12:8: "To one there is given . . . a message of knowledge by means of the same Spirit." In the case of discernment, God grants divine knowledge to an individual—things that couldn't be known by the person through any other means.[2]

"Deacon Brown, God allowed John and his father to be in the room alone, and I believe it was because someone needed to ask for forgiveness."

"You might have received a word of knowledge. That happens to me. Sometimes, you might not like what the Spirit shows you about a situation, person, or thing. Sometimes, you don't even want to know these things."

"Yes. In fact, I agree that this is what happened at the hospital."

"When that happens, you're supposed to pray for the person or situation."

"I'll do that." Then I told Deacon Brown, "I recently saw a quote by Corrie Ten Boom: 'Discernment is God's call to intercession, never to faultfinding.'"

I appreciated our conversation; however, this wasn't the only lesson God was teaching me about discernment. There is also a gift of discerning of spirits given by the Spirit based on 1 Cor 12:10 ("to another distinguishing between spirits"). Through the work of the Spirit, the revelation of good and evil spirits is made known.[3]

For example, there was a time when I attended a worship service at a large church in Detroit with a friend. During the service, I happened to look at the keyboardist's face. It didn't look normal. His face was distorted, but when I looked a second time, it did look normal. I couldn't believe what I had experienced.

The Holy Spirit had revealed to me that the keyboardist was not who he appeared to be. I believed I had seen an evil spirit. Later, I asked the friend who'd been sitting next to me if she noticed anything unusual about the keyboardist's face. She hadn't seen anything. I do not often tell anyone about this experience because it seems unbelievable and bizarre. It is easy to forget the presence of evil in our midst, but this was a reminder. I prayed for the keyboardist's deliverance from oppression and bondage.

God gives us what we need. He was developing my character, particularly patience. Sometimes, my patience went right out of the window. For instance, I once called my parents on Thanksgiving Day, one of my favorite holidays. I liked sitting together at the dining room table with them and praising God for his goodness.

---

2. Horton, *Gifts of the Spirit*, 39–40.
3. Horton, *Gifts of the Spirit*, 69.

However, during this period, a simple phone call to say I was coming over for Thanksgiving turned sour. When my mom answered the phone, I jokingly said, "I'm coming over. I know you guys aren't doing anything."

She said, "Don't make me upset."

That hadn't been my intent, but her response caused me to shut down, and I decided to stay home.

My cousin Cheryl called me later, and I told her what had happened. Cheryl encouraged me to go to my parents' house anyway. I sensed the Spirit leading me to get out of the hole I'd dug for myself and go.

When I got to their house, my parents and Frank, my brother, were happy to see me. Shortly after my arrival, we filled our plates with food and sat at the dining room table. Frank returned to his bedroom, where he had been watching Detroit's Thanksgiving parade as he did every year.

Before we left the table, I suggested having a Bible study, which turned into a precious moment.

Daddy said, "Let's read Daniel 3, the story about Shadrach, Meshach, and Abednego." They were put in the fiery furnace for not worshiping a pagan god, an image of gold.

After we'd read the passage, I asked, "Daddy, what would you title your message about this story?"

"I would have a subject of 'He's Able.'"

As I reread Dan 3:17–18, Dad's sermon title led me to believe his resilience came from knowing that in the most challenging circumstances, God *can* rescue us, whether he does or not. The three young Hebrew boys had known God was able to save them before they were put in the fiery furnace. It wasn't an afterthought.

I said my sermon title would be "Who's in the Fire with You?"

As I reread Dan 3:24–25, my sermon title led me to believe my resilience came from knowing that God had been with me all the time during my difficult circumstance of being unemployed. He hadn't changed the situation, but he kept me from being harmed. God was the fourth one Nebuchadnezzar saw in the furnace and said he looked "like a son of the gods." Shadrach, Meshach, and Abednego saw God in the furnace with them. I trust that I will see God in my fiery trials. I don't have to run from them because I will not be alone. God is not only a rescuer, but he is also a protector.

After the discussion about sermon titles, Mom said, "Let's read Psalm 91." Although she didn't have a sermon title, we read and discussed each verse. She mainly focused on verses 1 and 2. She said, "When we dwell in his secret place, he will protect us. I trust him." Dad and I agreed.

My nephew stopped by as we were finishing. I shared the good news of Jesus Christ with him to conclude our day. Mom was pleased that I had come over. I was, too. I reached and gave Mom and Dad a hug and kiss. I left at ten thirty at night. This sacred, precious, and enjoyable time together was indeed a Thanksgiving!

God continued to stretch me beyond my comfort zone and use me in service. I was invited to teach the Wednesday evening Sunday school teachers' class. In my studies, I used several commentaries and took a lot of notes to share. The Spirit exposed a blind spot. A desire to please people who knew more about the Bible than I did was revealed to me. Often, I recall this admonishment because I can't flow in the Spirit if I'm satisfying my flesh by trying to impress people. I don't want to ever ignore this reminder from the Spirit. I couldn't possibly flourish if I were trying to impress people, especially the ones God was preparing me to minister to.

I'd made an appointment to meet with Dr. Sampson to share a ministry proposal for women to know and be reminded of the love of Jesus Christ and our hope in him. While preparing the proposal, I had made a list of four qualified women teachers/speakers who could give a biblical message weekly at a women's shelter. I did not have peace about contacting them, although I wanted to. I knew that God wanted me to lead and give the message, but I wanted to pass it off to someone else. I struggled at first to accept God's will, and I was also afraid not to. He told me that he was going to do something new through me. I believed him. Dr. Sampson approved and blessed this new women's outreach ministry.

I phoned Chaplain Williams, an ordained minister in the United Methodist Church. She served a halfway house, the Grateful Home, with food and housing for women in Detroit. We met a couple of months later. Chaplain Williams, a stout African American woman with a serious look on her face, met me at the front door.

I told her I wanted to bring a Tabernacle Missionary Baptist Church team to minister to the women through a Bible lesson and songs. I said, "The Holy Spirit is going to touch their hearts. They will weep in the presence of God." I perceived her skepticism, although she nodded in agreement. I imagined she thought, "Right. Who does she think she is, saying what the Holy Spirit is going to do?" I was sincere and confident in God's mission.

On the day of our visit, the pianist couldn't make up her mind about joining us. Two hours before the service, I called Marcia, another pianist, and picked her up before stopping to get my friend Doris, who had volunteered to serve on our team. We prayed for God's protection and guidance in the service. Doris stepped forward and said she would drive. That gave me a chance to quiet my spirit and pray for the power of the Holy Spirit.

When we arrived at the Grateful Home, our team of eight was there and ready to serve. The first pianist hadn't shown up. Our hearts were open in our worship and the honoring of God for his goodness. Marcia's musical leadership brought us into God's presence. She was a gifted vocalist and worship leader.

Little did I know that I would preach. I mean, really preach. I gave an exposition of John 4 where Jesus and the Samaritan woman met at the well and brought my testimony about Jim witnessing to me about having an intimate, personal relationship with Jesus. I extended an invitation to meet Jesus at the well. I was preaching. I believed this was the something new God was doing. I didn't plan it, but God did, and the women were ready to receive.

I witnessed the presence of the power of the Holy Spirit overwhelming everyone. It was like a wave of the Spirit's presence from the back to the front of the large room. I remember seeing many women weeping before God, including Chaplain Williams and our volunteers. Women were hugging, holding each other, and dancing in the Spirit. Chaplain Williams said she had never seen anything like this before. I hadn't either—a release, a setting free. Five young women came forward to give their lives to Jesus. We praised the Lord!

God expanded our borders because of our first experience at the Grateful Home. Chaplain Williams gave us regular opportunities to return there and to serve at two other locations—Genesis II and the Detroit Rescue Mission. God gave us enough volunteers to meet the increase. The men and women in the three housing facilities were not ashamed to tell their stories about what God had done for them. Not only did they build each other up by talking about the goodness of God, they blessed the Tabernacle Baptist volunteers.

Today, the Grateful Home has expanded its services beyond food and shelter to social services and counseling. It is the oldest program serving

Oh, Taste and See!

chemically addicted women in Michigan. We were blessed to be part of their history.[4]

Around this time, I phoned my father to invite him to the Corinthian Baptist Church in Hamtramck, Michigan, where I was a visiting, evening Sunday school teacher from Tabernacle Missionary Baptist Church. Dad accepted. I remembered how he and I used to attend Corinthian Baptist together in past years. I thought it would be good for him to go back. The pastor and many others were glad to see him. A crowd of about fifty people came out for a quarterly learning event that each visiting church participated in once a year.

I didn't intentionally set out to start preaching toward the end of teaching the Sunday school lesson. I had been preaching in my dreams for a while and as planned, at the Grateful Home, but not spontaneously. As the lesson unfolded, though, it just happened that night, and the group was receptive.

When my dad and I walked to the car afterwards, he asked, "When did you learn to preach like that?"

I responded, "I've been studying God's word, and he's giving me opportunities to use my gifts."

He smiled like a proud dad. I'd seen that smile many times before. It was like a blooming flower, taking its time to unfold. I felt something profound in that moment because Dad had hoped my brother would be a minister. I'll never forget what I felt when Dad questioned me; I was thrilled to be his "preaching daughter."

God continued to grow me in new ways, using my God-given spiritual gifts. I attended a Women's Prayer Gathering at Tabernacle Church on a Saturday morning. As we gathered in the multipurpose room, about fifty women were led by the host in singing, "He Is Lord." We worshiped in God's presence. I heard chairs moving as we spontaneously stood to acknowledge his lordship. I loved it.

Our leader asked for women to come forward to pray before the teaching about prayer began. I sensed the Holy Spirit telling me to go forward. I tried convincing the Spirit to send my friend Lonetta because she could pray better than me. She always had the right words to pray. She didn't fumble over her words or pause too long between sentences. But the Spirit wouldn't listen to me. The Spirit said, "No, I want you to go." I felt like I had no choice but to go to the microphone to pray.

---

4. Berkholz, "Synopsis of Talk."

The presence of the Holy Spirit came over me as I began praising the Lord. And then these words were spoken through me:

> My little children, I love you so much. I want to do so many things for you. You have not given yourselves to me. Surrender. You're holding back areas of your life. You're in bondage. There's a spirit of jealousy among us.

I cried. I was shocked. I rushed out of the room to the kitchen and praised the Lord. If the woman who was to initially lead this prayer event had been there, I knew it would have been received differently because she grew up in a Pentecostal church where all the gifts of the Spirit are welcomed, and she was familiar with them. A few ladies approached me in the kitchen to see if I was all right.

After I got myself together, I returned to the event. A young lady from the Word of Faith Church in Detroit came to me. She said, "I know what happened. I understood and agreed with that word of prophecy." Her church operated in the spiritual gifts, as described in the Bible.

The next day Emily, who had attended the event, said, "Denise, do you know what happened?"

"Yes."

"You prophesied. I do not believe the women knew what was happening." Today, Rev. Dr. Emily Pardue still remembers what had happened that day.

I heed Dr. Sampson's wisdom today. He had said in a sermon, "You had better watch it when you get up to say something. People respect your integrity." I pray for God to keep me from standing up with prophetic messages if my words are not his words. I continue to ask for his assurance and encouragement that I'm not speaking from my flesh.

Not only did I learn about and practice publicly my God-given spiritual gifts, I learned privately also. One time, before I went to bed, I was writing in my journal, and I came to a point where it was as if God wrote his words guiding my hand. I didn't think about what to write; the words flowed from my pen:

> The gift I have given you cannot be purchased. The blood of my Son was shed on Calvary to save a wretch like you. I have redeemed you, chosen, and called you to serve me. You will begin to experience the freedom that comes from being my child. Open your heart and receive my manifold blessings. For I will fill your cup and use you to glorify me. You will not lack if you remain

humble before me. Turn not to the left nor to the right. The Holy Spirit will lead and guide you. Believe, my child, what I am doing in your life. Don't be afraid. Continue to lift me up before others. I will use you if you make yourself available to me. Be faithful in small as well as great things. O taste and see that the Lord is good.

God's words nourished my soul. I wondered if this way in which God revealed himself was a spiritual gift. We hadn't discussed it in any of my Bible classes, so I phoned my spiritual companion, Dr. Grace Moreman, who taught a class on the gifts of the Spirit, to find out what my experience was called.

She said, "Baby, that's called intimacy with God."

It was God's way of drawing me closer to him. I indeed had an intimate relationship with God. I had devoted time to listening, reflecting, getting to know, and being known by God. John 10:27 says, "My sheep hear my voice, and I know them, and they follow me." One time, my friend Emily said to the women in a gathering, "Denise marches to a different drumbeat." I resonated with this because I try to discern what God is saying. Later, I learned from Henri Nouwen's book *Discernment* that "when we are truly listening, we come to know that God is speaking to us, pointing the way, showing the direction." Nouwen continues, we are "breaking cadence with conventional thinking (what the Bible calls the 'spirit of the world'), listening to a different beat (intuition), and stepping to the music you hear (courage)."[5]

God was using me in ministry in new ways. I was learning to listen and to pay attention. My two and a half years of teaching primarily third graders had been a bittersweet experience, but I obeyed God's call. Now, I believed God was building my confidence in trusting him and using my God-given spiritual gifts.

One night at home, I spent time praying in my bedroom before falling asleep. I had an impression that it was time to sell my house and go to seminary in Columbia. The nudge came unexpectedly. The time was now. I was not going to use the same realtor. The next day, I phoned my spiritual companion, Dr. Moreman, who was also a realtor. She was a longtime teacher at Tabernacle Church and in the Detroit Public Schools. She agreed.

I prayed and asked God for three conditions to be met: my house would sell within a week, it would be with conventional financing, and I would get the price I asked for. I shared these conditions with Dr. Moreman. God answered all three conditions. It sold in four days.

---

5. Nouwen, *Discernment*, 176–77.

It was now three years after my initial contact with Columbia International University. The seminary had eliminated the master's level intercultural studies track, which I had planned to pursue; instead, I chose the MDiv program in the pastoral leadership track without hesitation.

The three-year delay was part of my spiritual formation. God was teaching me to trust him, to be available for service, and to learn for myself how spiritual gifts work. I could depend on the Holy Spirit to enable and equip me to flourish in God's kingdom. My loving God was building my character in patience, courage, and compassion. My Holy God was deepening my love relationship and faith in him. I was continually reminded of the beauty of my family and church communities. My God was maturing me in preparation for what I would further learn at CIU.

I looked forward to setting foot again on CIU's campus in the fall and to being there for the next three years. I never gave up on God because he never gave up on me. He was faithful. At last, he gave me the peach cobbler that I had been waiting for! I had tasted and seen that the Lord is good.

STONE OF REMEMBRANCE: FAITHFULNESS

As I prepared for the second time to go to seminary, I was reminded of all the ways God had used me as I waited for the peach cobbler—how he taught me and transformed me through this waiting period. "He who calls you is faithful; he will surely do it" (1 Thess 5:24). Waiting has a divine purpose.

REFLECTION QUESTIONS

Look back over your life to see times when you had to wait for what you thought you were ready for, but God let you know he had something else in mind. What is your peach cobbler? What did you learn after receiving it? In what ways do you celebrate now that you've received what you had been waiting for? Alone or with others? What is your stone of remembrance?

8

Grace on the Obstacle Course

God gives [grace] where he finds empty hands. —Augustine

When I had finished my first year in seminary, it felt good to turn in all course assignments and pack my belongings into the dorm storage unit. It had been refreshing to meet, study, and pray with sisters and brothers from various parts of the world. Among others, there were natives and missionaries from Kenya, Tanzania, Korea, Indonesia, Germany, and New Zealand. The professors and staff were approachable and always willing to give assistance. It was a welcoming and hospitable community.

I was grateful for God's love and care for me. As I prepared to leave for home, I recalled an early example of his care. When I went to turn in my first assignment for Introduction to Missions one evening, I had just ten minutes before it was to be in Dr. Mulholland's drop-off box. I hurried to the grad building. I introduced myself to a lady who was leaving as I was walking up the steps to the building. Her name was Cathy. I didn't know she was Dr. Mulholland's administrative assistant. I got my paper turned in on time, and I had met a new staff member.

The next day, I went to the Student Center to check my mailbox. I opened an unstamped envelope addressed to me. Cathy had written me a lovely note saying that after we met yesterday the Lord had brought my name to her mind several times. She didn't know why, but Cathy and her husband would be praying for me regularly while I was in seminary. I was reminded that "the effectual fervent prayer of a righteous man availeth much" (Jas 5:16 KJV). I didn't realize then how much I would need intercessors other than those already praying for me, like my home church prayer partners. God met my need in an unexpected way, as "he promises to meet all our needs according to his riches in glory in Christ Jesus" (Phil 4:19).

My first summer back home with my parents in Detroit was much needed. I hurried along to the departure gate to board my connecting plane at Hartsfield-Jackson International Airport. Onboard my flight, I placed my carry-on luggage in the overhead compartment. I had no idea the kind of experience that awaited me on the Delta flight 1619. Before boarding, I had wondered who my seatmate would be. Would they talk, sleep, watch a movie, or do something else?

I said, "Excuse me." The gentleman in the aisle seat stood so I could take the window seat. Sitting next to another African American didn't happen often. The flight attendants were instructed to prepare the cabin for takeoff. As I had many other times, I looked inside my traveling handbag to pull out my small black Bible to read a few Scriptures before takeoff and quietly pray for a safe flight.

After praying, my seatmate said, "I noticed your Bible. If you don't mind, what were you reading?"

I said, "I normally read Psalm 91 before a flight. I like to remind myself of God's presence and protection."

"I love the psalms. Are you a Christian?"

"Yes, I am. What about you?" I didn't want to make any assumptions, but I was open to talking, even if he wasn't a Christian.

We waited to speak again until the plane reached its cruising altitude, so we could hear each other better. I noticed my seatmate was wearing a dark suit jacket, had a neat, low haircut, and warm, brown-framed glasses to match his medium-brown complexion. He had a book in his lap.

He said, "I'm Reverend Jackson. Glad to meet you. I'm a retired pastor and an adjunct professor at an evangelical seminary."

"Oh, nice. I'm in a MDiv program in pastoral leadership at Columbia International University in Columbia, South Carolina. I'm Denise Posie."

"What year are you in, and why Columbia?"

"I just finished my first year." I shared with Reverend Jackson my interest in being in a multicultural environment with an emphasis on local and global missions. He listened as I highlighted fellowshiping with international students, adjusting to campus life, and being one of four female MDiv pastoral leadership program students.

"All right. So, what's challenging for you?"

"My studies are challenging, but I'm doing well. Maintaining my quiet time with the Lord is hard at times. Finding a church in a new city isn't easy either. Although this is not a challenge, I'm concerned about going into debt in this season of my life."

At forty-one, I knew this wasn't the best time to have unnecessary debt hanging over my head. I was totally relaxed about sharing my journey with a stranger. This was quite unusual, as normally people tell me their situations.

Then I surprised myself by saying, "I don't know if I want to go back."

Like a concerned pastor, he said, "Don't quit. God has a hedge around you. He will impart what you need by placing you in the path of people who have what you need. He's going to bless you for what you've done." Reverend Jackson spoke gently, pastorally, and prophetically. I knew God was speaking to me through him. He was saying what God wanted me to know—that he is God, and he's got this!

Speechless, and with a meeting of the eyes, I said, "Thank you for those words. They mean so much to me." Through his words, God had just encouraged me to remain faithful by staying in school. I gave Reverend Jackson my parents' address so he could send me reading resources over the summer.

At thirty-four thousand feet in the air, I sensed the closeness of God in the holy skies. I was in awe of his presence and peace, greatness and power, wisdom and foreknowledge. God had a plan for my life. Nothing escaped him, and he was in the details. It felt like a cool splash of water had been poured on me, refreshing me.

Our pilot made a perfect landing. Reverend Jackson and I walked side-by-side through the doorway to the arrival gates. We hugged as if we'd known each other for longer than an hour and a half.

"Goodbye, for now. I'll send a package soon."

"Thank you so much. It was a blessing to meet you, Reverend Jackson."

I made the long walk from the gate to the baggage claim area, fired up by this God encounter to stay the course, no quitting. I saw Reverend Jackson heading in the opposite direction. As I waited for my luggage, I thought about the impact his words had on me. Later, I would realize they had an even greater impact than I knew at the time, and it occurred to me that he might not ever know of their long-term effect on my life.

I was glad to be home, and my parents were happy to see me. Several days later, I opened the front door and found a large FedEx envelope from Reverend Jackson, addressed to me in lovely cursive penmanship. I couldn't wait to see what was inside. I carefully cut along the outer edges. When I saw the lovely, oversized card with its painting called *Dream Cottage* by Egidio Antonaccio, I gasped. Various colors of daisies—white, shades of pink, yellow and purple—with lots of greenery frame the entrance to a cottage. The surrounding trees are dense, tall, and wild. A stream runs under a knee-high white bridge leading to a cobblestone path to the elegant, peaceful cottage.

Inside the card, Reverend Jackson had written,

> Denise Posie, Dear Beautiful Woman and Precious Minister, it was both a blessing and a pleasure to meet you last Sunday on Delta Flight 1619. *The steps of a good man (woman) are ordered by the Lord*, Psa 37:23a. Denise, the sacrificial passion that you exhibit for the gospel of Christ, Rom 1:16, and the work of the ministry, Eph 4:12, is a very special gift that only Jesus can give. You are going to do great things, and God is going to use you mightily. Be encouraged and always remember:
>
> To walk with Jesus, no strength is lost
> To talk with Jesus, no breath is lost
> To wait on Jesus, no time is lost
> To work for Jesus, no pay is lost
> To suffer for Jesus, no crown is lost
> Walk on, pray on, wait on, work on, and press on.
> You are for always in all-ways in my prayers.
>
> Signed Rev. Jackson

Warm feelings came over me as I repeatedly read these powerful words and let them sink in. Proverbs 16:24 says, "Gracious words are a honeycomb, sweet to the soul and healing to the bones." The back of the card stated that the garden surrounding the dream cottage is intended to "evoke feelings of strength, beauty, grace, and wonderment."[1] I prayed for the Holy Spirit to evoke these feelings in my soul, and I responded, "Hallelujah!"

I asked for forgiveness for my lack of faith. I trusted God to enlarge my footsteps so my feet would not slip. I meditated on Ps 37:23–24: "The Lord makes firm the steps of the one who delights in him; though he may stumble, he will not fall for the Lord upholds him with his hand."

---

1. Antonaccio, *Dream Cottage*.

It was nourishment to my soul to imagine myself dancing in the presence of God, wearing a royal purple, flowing gown of fine linen, my feet bare among the flowers in Antonaccio's garden. I felt the warmth of the ground on my feet. I looked up and saw the Lord watching over his garden. He saw me, and I cried, "How majestic is your name." I sensed God's strength, beauty, grace, and wonder in my soul.

As I sat down, I was reminded of my favorite garden story in the Bible, where Jesus prayed earnestly in the garden of Gethsemane until he resolved in his heart that God's will be done. As followers of Jesus, we are invited to the garden to bring all our cares and burdens. We should leave only when God's will is resolved in our hearts.

In my imaginary garden, where I danced and prayed, God gave me water to strengthen and restore my soul. I placed Reverend Jackson's lovely card on the table; I wanted nothing but God's will. I left the garden.

I don't have a garden per se, but now I have a forty-five-minute drive to Lake Michigan, my go-to place. When I have difficult decisions to make, I sometimes feel the lake calling me, drawing me to itself. It's a place where God speaks to me, as he did in my imaginary garden. He strengthens me and fills me with his Spirit to face whatever circumstances I am faced with. Then, I leave the lake.

It was such a joy to be back on campus for my second year. Reverend Jackson's encouraging words made me excited about returning to CIU. I had made history by becoming the first black female resident assistant (RA) for graduate women in the Walker Residence Hall. Walker Hall's basement floor had a combination of traditional grad students, nontraditional (meaning older) grad students, and a few undergrad women. There was one African American student besides me and several non-white international students. The rest of the residents were white.

I was honored to be part of the dean's team to encourage, advise, and support grad women. I loved getting up early in the morning to open the lobby curtains so the residents could see outside before walking to the Student Center for breakfast. I cherished leaving a personal note with an accompanying Scripture verse on the room doors. I liked taping inspirational Bible verses on communal bathroom mirrors. I enjoyed gathering with the students in the lobby or someone's room for prayer and fellowship. We sipped fine tea and ate dainty cookies or chocolates from different countries. I relished spontaneous conversations and counseling opportunities. My cup was filled at the RA team retreats during the year.

However, not everything was easy. I've learned since that being the first woman in any role of responsibility often includes complications along with the joys.

One of the students on the basement floor, a young white woman, a first-year grad student, stood out. She had a high-octane personality and a warm, friendly smile. Her voice was easily distinguished in a group. She was interested in going to the mission field after her seminary training. During the first week of the fall semester, I asked Sophie to become one of our floor leaders for the year, which meant she would meet with the others regularly for prayer and fellowship in the lobby. If anyone needed a companion to pray or talk with them, the floor leader could be available for her. Sophie was eager to team up with the other grad floor leader.

The floor leaders and I met regularly for prayer and fellowship. We were inspired and in one accord as a team. For a time, everything went well, but then things shifted. I noticed that Sophie had stopped scheduling gatherings for prayer and inspiration. Her zeal wore off, and the other women met, but there was no Sophie. I vaguely remember talking to her about the sudden change in her behavior. She had other interests.

Late at night I began to hear the sounds of women walking through Walker Hall to their rooms, laughing and talking loudly, without consideration of our quiet hour observance. The disturbances turned out to be coming from Sophie and two of her friends, Joann and Laura. When I went out to ask Sophie and her friends to keep their voices down, they snickered and kept walking. A couple of weeks after the latest of several incidents, I heard knocking on my window one night, accompanied by the same snickering voices. They had run away before I could get outside.

Joann lived in one of the other dorms, but Laura, a quiet young white woman, lived in Walker. She seemed to be a closer buddy to Sophie than Joann, and this was her first year. Joann was a leader, a former RA, now a second-year student. She was also white and a little older than Sophie and Laura. Joann, too, was mission-field bound. This trio of rabble-rousers continued to disrespect and ignore my requests of them.

When I saw Guat, a mature friend from Malaysia, on campus one day, I shared with her what was going on in Walker.

She said, "You're in a parenting position. They're testing you."

That same day, I went with my friend Judy to the Men's Open Dorm—the only time the opposite sex was allowed there. Streamers, balloons, games, posters, and music were part of the fun night. I shared my situation with Judy as we walked together. Judy shared some additional words of wisdom with me. She said, "Pray especially for Sophie. Denise, this is preparation for your involvement in a congregation in the future." I was still thinking about what Guat had said about parenting. "I haven't raised any children," I thought. Both friends were experienced mothers.

At times, I would've given the people involved in a volatile situation a piece of my mind, but God spoke to me clearly, "I want you to be silent." I heard my inner voice say, "What?" I thought about Isa 1:18: "Come, now let us reason together." I understood God was telling me not to defend myself. Let it go. I did. I left it with God. Today, I will rarely defend myself. This is another lesson God taught me.

I learned to take a "licking and kept on ticking." The Village Idiom says the phrase originated in the United States, dating to the mid-twentieth century, and it means that despite how challenging the situation is that you find yourself in, you endure and persevere.[2]

I know now how important it is for people, especially in ministry, to take responsibility for their behavior—appropriate and inappropriate. Today I am a trained consultant in managing conflict, and I understand how better processes could have been used. I see that I, too, could have done better.

With only three weeks remaining in the semester, things got quieter on the Walker basement floor.

I served in my RA role until the end of the year, but I decided not to continue as an RA or to live on campus. I needed time to heal. That experience turned out to be the most painful and informative time of my seminary years; it taught me so much that would, as my friends had suggested, put me in a good position in my life in church ministry.

My spiritual formation in seminary deepened my knowledge and intimacy with God for a lifetime. Then, and now, I live by CIU's motto, "To know Him and to make Him known." My heart, mind, and hands were opened to receiving God's grace on the obstacle course in new ways. God sent a messenger, and I believed. God gave me intercessors, and I benefited from the prayers of the righteous. God spoke to me, and I obeyed. God warned me, and I paid attention. God fought my battle, and I submitted to his will. God gave me a testimony, and I shared it. By his grace, I followed him. Although I have been tempted at different points, I didn't stray or take alternative paths.

2. Village Idiom, "Take a Licking."

In both situations, the Delta flight and Walker Hall, God's grace was given, and I was willing to receive. I trusted God. My decision to go back to seminary was personal, and it only affected me. On the other hand, my decision concerning Walker Hall was personal and collective; it affected more than me. Yet, in both situations I was given God's grace. It can be easy to miss God's grace in a difficult situation, but I was ready to receive; my hands were empty.

STONE OF REMEMBRANCE: GRACE

I took it to heart when God told me to be silent and not defend myself concerning this matter. It was God's grace that kept me strong and hopeful that this, too, would pass. God fights our battles. He taught me a common practice to not defend myself, particularly in sensitive situations. "And God is able to bless you abundantly, so that in all things at all times, having all that you need, you will abound in every good work" (2 Cor 9:8). God's grace sustains us.

REFLECTION QUESTIONS

Thinking back, was there a time when God gave you enough grace to trust him without your intervention or help in fixing a situation? How did you respond? What lifelong lessons did you learn and remember? What is your stone of remembrance?

9

The Unfolding of an Undeniable Conviction

One of the most difficult disciplines in the period of transition is waiting for the new door to open. —Ben Campbell Johnson

In the summer of 1997, after completing my RA responsibilities, I packed my belongings and moved into the beautiful home of Mrs. Walker, a well-established African Methodist Episcopal Church member. It didn't work out for me after I'd lived there for three months because I felt isolated and restricted in my limited space, an upstairs medium-sized bedroom across from a bathroom with no shower. The filled closets and drawers left little room for my things. I enjoyed our time together at the table for a meal. I didn't enjoy not meeting our neighbors, other than the people next door, because everyone came in and out of their garages straight into their houses.

My friend Judy wasn't surprised when I told her I needed to find a new place. Because she was going out of town, she offered me her off-campus trailer for a night. It was a perfect weekend getaway to relax, although the power went out in our area that evening. In the dark, quiet night, I asked the Lord about having a place like Judy's. At the same time, I asked for the right person to live with Mrs. Walker. On Monday, Judy and I went down the street from CIU to see Mrs. Vincent, who owned several trailers and small apartments near the seminary. She didn't have any vacancies and didn't expect any. I was disappointed but willing to patiently wait.

When I returned to Mrs. Walker's house after preaching at the State Park Correctional Center a couple of weeks later, I had gotten a message from Mrs. Vincent. Surprisingly, a student in one of the two affordable small apartments in front of Judy's trailer had to leave school due to a family situation, and he didn't know if or when he would return. I went to Mrs. Vincent's house to pay the deposit. It was perfect for me. I moved in and loved living there, except for one thing: Judy told me to watch out for snakes at night. I never saw one, but the thought of them kept me on my toes, looking out for them in the dark.

In the spring of 1998, I was invited to give a testimony on love in a CIU chapel service. I was grateful for the opportunity to share, but I didn't have anything in mind that I would talk about. Right afterwards, when I got to my apartment, the phone rang. It was my mom. I knew something was wrong.

She asked, "Where are you?"

"Columbia, South Carolina," I said.

"What are you doing there?"

"I'm studying in seminary."

"Oh." I could hear Ruthie's voice in the background.

"Let me speak to Ruthie."

"Denise wants to talk to you." Ruthie is a longtime friend from my parents' hometown who often visited our family and would stay with my brother if needed. I wondered what was going on.

"Ruthie, is something going on with my mom? Does she have a memory problem?"

"Yes." She burst into tears when she told me both my parents had memory issues.

"Put my mother back onto the phone." I couldn't hold back my tears. I stopped when my mom rejoined me.

I said, "Mom, I'm going to come home to care for you and Dad." I knew deep down that Mom knew herself that something was wrong because she never said why she had called in the first place. It was God's grace that my mother called. I booked a reasonable flight to Detroit, departing on the following Monday. I was reminded of God's faithfulness always.

In the meantime, I prayed as I prepared a short chapel testimony. In my Greek class on Thursday afternoon, Professor Harvey translated 1 John 4:11–15, and it was impressed in my spirit to give a testimony about how "God Is Perfecting Love in Me," based on verses 16–18:

The Unfolding of an Undeniable Conviction

And so, we know and rely on the love God has for us. God is love. Whoever lives in love, lives in God, and God in them. This is how love is made complete among us so we will have confidence on the day of judgment: In this world, we are like Jesus. There is no fear in love. But perfect love drives out fear.

The following morning, I sat in quietness before the Lord in my comfy living room chair where I often read the Bible and prayed. Then I went to the chapel and stood before God's people. I admitted I had struggled to come up with something to say, but I had prayed for guidance. I wrote down several points on a three-by-five index card. I shared my testimony:

> God has dealt with me before regarding love and forgiveness. But since I've been at CIU, he has been perfecting his love in me. I didn't realize until now that God was using my experiences in the Richland Memorial Hospital Clinical Pastoral Education (CPE) for my spiritual formation. CPE allows the participant to minister to people from various faith traditions and circumstances without imposing their own beliefs on those they're working with. In the process, we grow in our own spiritual identity and self-awareness.
>
> My experiences at Richland included ministering to a white family when their son had been shot by a black man, to a patient with AIDS after talking myself into not being afraid, to a white Pentecostal pastor whose wife was dying, and to gang members who were expressively angry when their friend died from a gunshot wound upon arrival. Through these diverse experiences, God was perfecting his love in me. We don't know who God will call us to minister to. Some of you may have been raised to discriminate against certain people, but God didn't call us to pick and choose who we love and support. He wants us to love others, even when they don't meet our expectations.
>
> Two days ago, I received a call from my home in Detroit informing me that my mom and dad were ill. Sometimes I've been challenged being with my parents. I probably wouldn't have gone to check on them, if this had happened a year ago. I would have said, "I'm too busy getting to know God and making him known. I must finish school." But God is perfecting his love in me.
>
> Since I've been at CIU, I've grown to live in love and to live in God. Living in his love, we have an acceptance of all people. Living in his love, we minister from a nonjudgmental posture. We can't allow our fears about others or anything else to suppress living in his love. What's holding you back from loving others? If we leave CIU without having the capacity to love others, I'm afraid we've

missed the mark. God's perfect love drives out fear. What are you afraid of?

Please join me in prayer.

I lingered at the front of the chapel to greet people. Many students came up to wish me well and express appreciation for my testimony. I saw my friends, Yvonne and Laslene, approaching. I expressed to them how good I felt because I experienced the presence of the Holy Spirit as I shared my testimony.

On Monday, I caught my flight to Detroit. My time at home was filled with doctor's appointments, house cleaning, and chauffeuring my parents to the grocery store and other appointments. I felt they were taken care of and were doing well. We arranged that my sisters, who lived in Detroit, would regularly check on them. I left feeling encouraged and ready to return home, if necessary.

Looking back, I realize my experiences before and during my seminary days were part of the discernment process of my calling to ministry. I needed to be sure I heard God's call, not mine or someone else's. I didn't take God's summons lightly.

After completing the chaplaincy internship, I was encouraged to become a residential chaplain at Prisma Health Richland Hospital, formerly Richland Memorial. I had experienced God's grace as a chaplain serving a population of diverse races, ethnicities, communities of faith, and cultures; however, I wanted to be part of a larger community. I did interview for the position, but it was clearly not God's will for me, as the door closed.

A month before the chaplaincy interview, I became a member and served in an associate ministerial role at Saint John Baptist Church. I felt at home in this historical, large black church in the inner city with its choirs, where deacons led devotions at the beginning of the worship service, and I experienced warm hospitality. Pastor Wright welcomed my God-given gifts in presiding and sometimes preaching in worship services, and in developing a prayer ministry. It was a fruitful time, and I sensed again that God was preparing me for future ministry.

My calling to be a woman pastor and preacher unfolded into an undeniable conviction, which meant I would seek no vocational options other than the pastorate and preaching. God opened and closed doors as part of my discernment. I enjoyed this season in Columbia and decided to extend my seminary training by one semester and graduate at the end of spring 1999, a year later.

The Unfolding of an Undeniable Conviction

Another way God was preparing me for the next phase of my journey was through meaningful conversations with ordained women serving in the church, which still today, is male dominated. One of those conversations was with Diane, an associate pastor of a large, historical United Methodist Church in Columbia. This soft-spoken white woman said, "No matter what situations you find yourself in, stay focused on God's mission. You can't go wrong." I was drawn to paying close attention to the tone of her voice. I knew it was God speaking to me. Remembering Diane's words kept me from losing my focus many times later on.

One of those times was when I was asked to fill in for someone else at an affluent black Baptist church in the country near Columbia. I was invited to join Pastor Smith, associate ministers, and officers in his office for prayer before the worship service. I was informed by Pastor Smith to preach from the lectern instead of the pulpit. Like this church, typically, in the Baptist church, the announcements, recognition of visitors, and congregational prayers are made from the lectern. The pulpit is strictly used by ordained and licensed clergy to preach and lead worship.

He said, "Is that all right with you?"

I said, "Yes, that's fine. I will preach anywhere." I recalled Diane's advice to stay focused. I wasn't going to allow my flesh to get in the way of being used to share the gospel. God was calling me to preach.

In my reading and in the personal stories from others, I learned about several people in ministry who reported dreaming or waking up with an awareness they had been preaching in their sleep, when God was calling them into ministry. This was my experience also. I had other dreams, also related to my call. I took the liberty of sharing one of my dreams matter-of-factly with my pastor, Dr. Sampson of Tabernacle Missionary Baptist Church. I wasn't looking for an understanding or interpretation. I thought it was a strange dream. He listened intently as I shared.

I told him, "I was at Tabernacle on the third-floor balcony. I had run late for the Sunday morning worship service, which had already started. The doors to the main floor were closed, so I followed the people in front of me to the third floor. I looked around for something to help me out of my dilemma because I was supposed to be on the first floor. I discovered I was a superwoman with unusual powers. I grabbed a large sheet by its corner, tied it to a large hook on the ceiling, and zoomed down to the sanctuary on the first floor. Mark, the usher at the sanctuary door, recognized my superpower, as I landed firmly on both feet with everything intact. He smiled and graciously opened the door to let me into the sanctuary."

Dr. Sampson said, "You are breaking through the tradition of the doors being closed. They couldn't shut you out."

I said, "I had never seen it that way. I dismissed it as just a strange, silly dream."

Three years later, I had a dream with a similar meaning. This time, it directly involved Dr. Sampson. In the dream, he stepped from behind his desk to greet two large men who had come to his office to see him. Dr. Sampson was a tall, big man. The men caught him off guard and shoved his back against the front of a bookcase with beveled glass doors. Dr. Sampson didn't push back. He braced himself so he would not fall. But he rebuked them for what they had done. That was the end of my dream.

On a Saturday morning, I talked to my friend Audrey. She was a mature Christian woman who was also a teacher in the Detroit schools, and I shared my dream with her. She was immediately concerned about Dr. Sampson's safety. Audrey alluded to some unknown persons who wanted to harm our pastor.

She said, "We need to pray right now for Dr. Sampson."

I closed the classroom door, we joined hands, and she prayed. While Audrey was praying, the Holy Spirit gave me the interpretation of my dream.

I said, "Audrey, the Spirit revealed to me that Dr. Sampson was attempting to move forward with the ordination of women, but some officers were holding him back."

My third dream was unlike the others; the people in it were distinct, colorful, and united. I had been preaching to a large crowd of people from different races, nations, and walks of life. We sang, "Let All the Peoples Praise Him." Someone read Ps 67:5: "May the peoples praise you, God; may all the peoples praise you." It wasn't until later that I understood my dream through the lens of Rev 7:9: "After this I looked, and there before me was a great multitude that no one could count, from every nation, tribe, people and language, standing before the throne and before the Lamb." My dream was not necessarily about the local church; it reflected God's glorious kingdom here on earth. No matter where God called me, I would remember this vision of his kingdom—the universal church, one church!

I had no doubt that God had called me.

The Unfolding of an Undeniable Conviction

Referring again to the book *The Critical Journey* by Janet O. Hagberg and Robert A. Guelich, later in life I understood that at this part of my journey, I was in what the authors refer to as stage five, "The Journey Outward." When an individual shifts primarily from an inward focus to an outward focus, they are surrendered to God's will without fully knowing all the details of his purposes for them. In stage five, the individual has a steadiness not to be moved by external circumstances.[1] For me, at this point, I experienced a stronger sense of calling, a desire to relate to others out of a place of love and concern for their wellbeing, and an inner peace and certainty of God's presence. These characteristics of "The Journey Outward" were amplified and brought into a clearer focus, as my seminary training would soon end. All the time, God had been guiding me to this very moment.

God would soon introduce me to a new community reflecting his kingdom and glory. While checking my mailbox on campus, I found an invitation from Beverly, who worked in CIU's administration office. The first female chaplain in the United States Air Force was being honored at Shaw Air Force Base in Sumpter, South Carolina, which was less than an hour away. Beverly thought I might be interested in attending after hearing my testimony about the hospital chaplaincy. I thought this was unusual because I wasn't in the military, but I liked new experiences, and I had two military classmates who were also invited.

I proudly walked side-by-side with my military friends, who were in uniform, as we entered the white double doors of the Officers' Club at Shaw that morning for an all-day celebration honoring Chaplain Colonel Lorraine K. Potter, the first female in military chaplaincy. The keynote presentation was "Serving Others, God and Country: Partnership and Pluralism."

During a break, Chaplain Major Eddie Walters approached me and introduced himself. After introducing myself, I shared the story behind the invitation to this event. He asked what I planned to do after finishing seminary. I said, "Whatever God has in store." Chaplain Walters invited me to join him for lunch later. Of course, I agreed. My heart was open to whatever God wanted me to receive.

After lunch, Chaplain Colonel Potter told her story of acceptance into the Air Force in 1973, which was her heart's desire even though she had previously been rejected because women were not commissioned at that time. She would progress through higher service ranks until she retired in 2004 as a major general. My takeaway from the event was to be all you're

---

1. Hagberg and Guelich, *Critical Journey*, 134.

called to be wherever you serve. I liked the chaplain's focus on "being" because what we do flows from who we are. Our "being" will affect how we serve all kinds of people. She gave an elevator pitch for recruiting chaplains. I wondered if this was the reason I'd been invited to attend. It became clear that it wasn't; I was one year too old to enlist.

I didn't know it then, but I was there to meet Chaplain Major Walters. Walters, an alumnus of Howard School of Divinity, a historically black university (HBCU), said he received ministry announcements from Howard regularly and would forward them to me. I was elated and grateful for a new experience and connection.

Weeks later, I received a large envelope from Chaplain Walters with several ministry announcements. I flipped through the many job or ministry vacancies. Most were with Washington, DC, nonprofits. An assistant pastor position at a United Methodist Church in Minneapolis caught my attention because it was a large, multicultural congregation. I called, but the position had been filled. I left the envelope on the floor and went about my day. That evening, I went through the flyers again. I hadn't seen the flyer for a co-pastor at the Immanuel Christian Reformed Church in Kalamazoo, Michigan. The church is part of the Christian Reformed denomination based in Grand Rapids. I'd never heard of the denomination and knew little about Kalamazoo. I don't know how I had missed it the first time.

I went to the library to research the denomination's beliefs. Although I was familiar with the Protestant Reformation and John Calvin, I needed more. A shelf of journals caught my attention on my way out of the library. The *Calvin Theological Journal* was within two arm's-length of me, so I stopped and skimmed through the contents and a few pages. I noticed its scholarly, theological emphasis. But I kept searching. I wasn't ready to make the call yet.

I met with my academic advisor, Dr. William Larkins, who had got to know me quite well for almost three years. He always had my best interests in mind. He was a clergy in one of the largest Presbyterian denominations in the United States, the Presbyterian Church of America (PCA), which prohibited the ordination of women clergy. In addition, he had a passion and measure of grace for all women and African American seminarians. I was drawn to his love for Jesus, scholarship, and humility.

Dr. Larkins asked me a series of questions and listened to my desires and concerns. Then, as he slightly lowered his head, he said, "I think you should call them."

The Unfolding of an Undeniable Conviction

My drive home allowed time for me to think about the next step. I called Pastor Mark at Immanuel Church to express my interest in co-pastoring with him. He returned my call and was quite interested in getting to know me. I met the requirements set forth by the search committee, which would result in two teleconference calls, three in-between calls with Pastor Mark or the chair of council, and a church visit.

One of their requirements was for the candidate to preach one Sunday as part of the hiring process. I had told Pastor Mark about my upcoming ordination at Tabernacle Church on January 10, when I would be in Detroit. Pastor Mark asked if I would be willing to come to Immanuel to preach on Sunday, January 17, and have a conversation with the search committee. I agreed, even though it would be during some cold, wintry days, not so easy for getting around.

After I got to Detroit, I felt hurried in my preparations for the ordination. I had not been able to meet with the other four candidates to prepare in the fall. Tabernacle Missionary Baptist Church was one of only a few Baptist churches in the National Baptist Convention to ordain women at that time. A candidate for ordination at Tabernacle Church was required to successfully pass an oral examination before an appointed council, be actively involved in a leadership role in ministry, and be a member in good standing. The requirements for ordination were the same for women as for men.

I was blown away when Pastor Mark called Tabernacle and asked if I was there. I just happened to be at the church. He was checking to see if I was still coming and to wish me well for my ordination. He didn't have my parents' phone number but remembered my church's name. His call encouraged me and made quite an impression that I was following God's will. When I believe I'm doing God's will, he gives me the confidence to walk in his strength.

Time was winding down. Two days before the ordination, I asked my dad to pray for me while we were talking at the dining room table. I can only imagine what was going through his mind at the time because of what he said before praying. Dad said, "I was a failure in the ministry." I don't know why he would have said this, but I believe he didn't see the spiritual and physical growth he had hoped for in himself and his small congregation. As I have grown in my spiritual journey now, I believe success is defined by following God's will and leaving the results to him. This principle was taught to me by Dr. Charles Stanley of the First Baptist Church in Atlanta.

In Dad's prayer, he reminded me of God's faithfulness and grace—that he hadn't brought me this far to leave me. I felt sad because I believe my dad also might have said he was a failure because he couldn't support me as a new minister. He didn't have the experience at the level I would need. I am grateful, however, that my family would witness my ordination. They had been on this journey with me for nearly seven years, and we were getting closer to my destination.

The day I had been waiting for arrived. My parents, siblings, niece, friends, and I met at Tabernacle Church. Although we were early, Dr. Sampson was at the door as if he were waiting for us. I'll never forget how Dr. Sampson made my father feel by showing him respect and appreciation as a fellow brother and pastor in the Baptist tradition. Although Dr. Sampson was a renowned preacher on both a local and global scale and my father had been the pastor of a small, local congregation, Dr. Sampson treated him as an equal. As he commented on how blessed my parents were to have me as their daughter, I saw my father's face lift and his shoulders pull back. Dr. Sampson extended his head and hand forward as if to say thank you. My father's face lit up as if God was shining from inside him. It was a holy moment for me. I knew God was present, and everything was going to be all right.

My guests went into the sanctuary, and I went to the conference room for instructions and prayer. The ordination service began with opening songs, prayer, Old and New Testament readings, and Dr. Sampson's acknowledgment of the occasion. The ordinands, two women and three men, were escorted into the sanctuary one at a time as Dr. Sampson called each name. The audience applauded the nicely dressed men and women in our dark suits and polished shoes.

I appreciated the meditation solo, which came between the candidates' presentation and the sermon. Sister Cynthia Harrington sang "I'll Go." The song touched me profoundly, making me think about my commitment to God's call. Tears fell as I reflected on my call Scripture—Isa 6:1–8, specifically verse 8: "Whom shall I send? And who will go for us? And I said, 'Here am I. Send me!'"

Dr. Ned Adams spoke from Acts 9:10–18, Saul's conversion, and reminded us of what we needed to know about preaching. I noted three things God expected: the preacher (1) "operates in the power of God from a position of humility," (2) knows that "fear, doubt, and guilt are all Satan's

The Unfolding of an Undeniable Conviction

tools to delay and defer the purposeful intent of preaching," and (3) must always "preach Jesus Christ and him crucified for the world's salvation."

We were reminded of Paul's new understanding of what the Lord would do with his weaknesses as described in 2 Cor 12:9: "But he [the Lord] said to me, 'My grace is sufficient for you, for my power is made perfect in weakness.' Therefore I will boast all the more gladly about my weaknesses, so that Christ's power may rest on me." Later, I often reminded myself about the sufficiency of God's grace in my weaknesses. God doesn't send his ministers without preparing them well for his mission in the power of the Holy Spirit. We must pray for humility.

Following that powerful sermon, the examination of the ordinands in the presence of at least five hundred people would begin. The candidates made a sincere effort to answer questions about our calling, our understanding of biblical/theological doctrines, and the Baptist church polity and administration. Years later, I wished I had shared more about my call experiences—for example, dreams, prophecies, and an irresistible urge to preach. I can imagine my responses to the questions could have been more robust if I had more time for preparation. I was assured that I would be all right in my spirit.

I shared two events from my call experience. I said, "I told God in a dream that I didn't know how to preach. God said, 'Open your mouth, my child, and I will speak through you.'" I don't typically tell people this part of my calling because I'd heard people say that God won't just put the words in your mouth. I understand the importance of sermon preparation. I also mentioned preaching in my dreams while sleeping.

When we were finished responding to all their questions, the catechizer asked the council of thirty-three men and women ministers and pastors from Tabernacle and other Baptist and affiliate churches if there was one last question. A male pastor of the council responded, "Yes," and was directed to ask his question. He said, "We talk in the context of the Baptist tradition, and as we all know, historically, there has been a resistance to the notion of ordaining women in the Baptist tradition. All of you have expressed your calling experientially, but this is directed toward the two women. What is your biblical defense of your calling as a woman?"

Dr. Sampson immediately stood, and I perceived it as a sign of his spiritual authority as the pastor of Tabernacle Church. He wouldn't let them humiliate us or force our backs against the wall. I also looked over at a key leader of the ordination process, who was sitting in front of the ordinands next to the catechizer. He made eye contact with me and moved his lips, "Don't answer it."

The other woman ordinand, Jeri, had the mic. She asked the catechizer for permission to answer the question. She felt like she shouldn't have to defend her call, but out of respect to the questioner, she would. Jeri expounded on several key Scriptures: Gal 3:28, Joel 2:28, and Acts 2, including the last days as referenced in Joel's prophecy, "And it shall come to pass afterward, that I will pour out my spirit upon all flesh; and your sons and your daughters shall prophesy, your old men shall dream dreams, your young men shall see visions."

The people clapped loudly and said, "Yay," and "Hallelujah." Jeri looked at me and passed the mic. If someone had dropped a pin, you would have heard it.

The catechizer looked at me and said, "Reverend Posie."

I didn't have to think about my answer. I wasn't intimidated, afraid, or trying to be disrespectful. I was confident that I had an answer.

I said, "Ditto."

The audience spoke loudly, clapping, laughing, and saying, "Yay," and "Praise the Lord." I heard Dr. Sampson's voice over all the voices. I'm sure I didn't laugh, but I smiled lightly. It was a kairos moment, a divine interruption of what would normally happen.

The catechizer said, "Mr. Moderator, I now recommend that the council go into a closed session, and we will convene afterward." Dr. Sampson instructed a minister to take the candidates to his office.

The wait seemed long, at least twenty-five minutes, though I'm not sure. While we waited, the people sang several familiar hymns. I glanced at the ordination service program several times and noticed that the Women and Girls' Choir had sung "The Potter's House," led by two sisters, Geri Kitchen and Ruth White, while we waited in the office. I remembered my Old Testament lifetime Scripture, Isa 64:8 (KJV): "But now, O Lord, thou art our father; we are the clay, and thou our potter; and we all are the work of thy hand." When I lived in the dorm at CIU, Anna, a potential student, who was Chinese American, stayed two nights in my dorm room as part of her discernment process. When her stay was over, she gave me a card she had written in calligraphy with this Scripture. Since that time, it has become my Old Testament lifetime Scripture. I had also listed it as my favorite Scripture in the candidates for ordination section of the program. The song says, "The Potter wants to put you back together again." When I read that

The Unfolding of an Undeniable Conviction

this song was part of the program, I felt secure because I knew God always had his hand on me.

When our wait was over, a key leader of the ordination process read the council's report. "My brothers and sisters, you all have been waiting and praying for the results of the council. The council has unanimously voted that all the candidates be ordained for the gospel ministry." The audience broke out in praise and clapping. I turned my back to the audience with both hands pointing toward heaven, giving God praise and thanksgiving. A pastor prayed a Spirit-filled prayer as ordained ministers joined in laying hands on the newly ordained ministers.

After the ordination service, one of Tabernacle Church's ministers on staff, Reverend Green, said, "Denise, the Holy Spirit must have told you to say ditto." I understood what he meant; it was risky. I wasn't trying to be disrespectful or witty. I opened my mouth, and "ditto" came out. I realized it was a God word.

I was affirmed, and I embraced my calling and ordination. I've not denied or defended my calling ever. Dad got what he wanted—a preacher in the family. I got what God had already ordained for me.

STONE OF REMEMBRANCE: CALLING

God opened and closed doors. He taught me to listen and know his voice in whatever way he chooses to speak, and be mindful of distractions. God gave me a strong sense of calling, mobilizing me to follow the Spirit anywhere. God's calling is personal and collective; the body of Christ affirms us.

REFLECTION QUESTIONS

What are the circumstances and context of your calling? What did God do or say to you that kept you faithful in responding to his call, especially in a sensitive situation? What effect did it have on you and others? What did you learn or adopt as a practice? What is your stone of remembrance?

10

Now, That's Love

You have been loved into who you are and into your calling to ministry by so many people. Although you don't write about it, you have passed on to so many others the love that was given you. —Mark Scheffers

I accepted my friend Mary's offer to drive me to Kalamazoo on the Sunday following my ordination. It meant a lot to me that we could enjoy each other's company during the two-and-a-half-hour drive from her house. We had known each other for ten years and would now get a taste of southwest Michigan as residents from the state's east side. Finally, we came to our exit, the Highway 94 business loop. We commented on the quaint downtown with a few high-rises, a McDonald's restaurant, a gospel mission, and an elegant Radisson Plaza Hotel. The trees were beautifully draped in long, pencil-thin icicles. It was breathtaking.

We arrived at the beige and burgundy–trimmed brick church building with a large canopy over the entrance, on a prominent corner on the north side of Kalamazoo. The building had once been a Harding's grocery store until the late sixties and was then occupied by the Nation of Islam before Immanuel Church purchased it. As I learned in my later studies, the history of a church is vital to understanding its ministry context—including the land, the building, and the purpose of its existence. After driving around the city, I thought Kalamazoo could be my next home. Already that morning, I envisioned the church's neighborhood as a mission field for community development to include an after-school tutoring program.

This visit would be the first of two in-person visits to preach, meet with the search team, and eventually meet with the congregation so they could get to know my philosophy of ministry, personality, ministry experience, and my vision. I also wanted to know some of their longings and challenges in reaching the surrounding, predominately black community. Immanuel was primarily an ethnically Dutch congregation with a long history on the north side. Its heyday had been in the mid-eighties.

Pastor Mark and his wife, Patricia, had been missionaries in Liberia, Africa, before coming to Immanuel in 1991. During Pastor Mark's tenure, he had been a proponent of the Christian school staying in the inner city when, years earlier, whites left the north side for the suburbs.

I thought the Pastor of Evangelism and Ministries Development position, for which I was applying, was an opportunity for discipleship, reaching our neighbors, and getting involved in the greater Kalamazoo community. I easily imagined myself working with Pastor Mark because our gifts would be complementary. I perceived Mark as quiet, an introvert, precise, and set on cruise control, whereas I am excitable, an extrovert, spontaneous, and likely to go into overdrive at times. We would be able to appreciate our differences because we were both passionate about making disciples. I didn't think trust would be an issue because we were each secure in our spiritual gifts and callings—crucial for a pastoral team; at Immanuel, co-pastors would be coequal. Mark was knowledgeable about racial reconciliation, and I was also. I was interested in being part of this work on a deeper level, and I felt Immanuel Church and the Christian Reformed (CRC) denomination would further my understanding in this area. I was specifically interested in systemic or structural racism, although I didn't know what it was called at the time.

After the visit, my sister Deborah took me to the airport to return to Columbia; she said, "I think you're going to get a call to this church. God has blessed you to connect with people from all walks of life." I knew what she said encompassed race, socioeconomic status, single life or married, homelessness, lives touched by addiction, prison reentry, youth, age, and more.

Over the next three months, in addition to my visit, I met on two conference calls with the search committee so we could get to know each other better and discern whether there was a ministry match. I left those meetings encouraged and anticipated hearing from the committee within three weeks.

In the final phase of the search committee's work, it was determined that I had a stronger gift for evangelism than the other candidates. I was passionate then, and still am, about being used by God to lead the lost to Jesus Christ and to disciple them. I became more and more excited about the new position. The council flew me to Kalamazoo to preach a second time, to be presented to and have a chance to converse informally with the congregation. The congregation would take a vote at a later time.

After my dialogue with the people, there was a holy moment when Pastor Mark invited me and the congregation to form a circle at the front of the worship center. They sang "Seek Ye First," which includes the lyrics, "Seek ye first the kingdom of God and his righteousness, and all these things shall be added unto you." I didn't know the song, but Matt 6:33, which contains these words, was my New Testament lifetime Scripture.

I received a call from the council president, Elder Dieleman, in early May and learned that I had been voted as Immanuel Christian Reformed Church's new co-pastor by an overwhelming vote of 90 percent. I was overjoyed. Pastor Mark called to congratulate me. A week later, I received a letter of call and a position description.

Two beacons of light shone on me regarding Immanuel Church during my time of discernment. One day in April, at the CIU chapel service, Dr. John Perkins was our guest preacher. I was familiar with Dr. Perkins's community development philosophy through the organization he founded, the Christian Community Development Association. I had an opportunity to talk to him briefly while he was waiting in the lobby after his chapel message.

He asked me, "What will happen after you graduate from seminary?"

I said, "I'm being strongly considered for a co-pastor position at Immanuel Christian Reformed Church in Kalamazoo, Michigan."

He smiled and nodded. "Oh, the Christian Reformed Church. I've been coming to Grand Rapids [the church's headquarters] for many years. You should prayerfully consider going to Immanuel. There are good people in the Christian Reformed Church. Be sure to become good friends with the other co-pastor."

"I'm excited about serving in that church and in the denomination."

He smiled. "God will lead the way for you."

I looked forward to accepting or declining the letter of call after talking with my pastor, Dr. Sampson, who would send the second beacon of light during my time of discernment. A week had passed since I had asked to speak with Dr. Sampson, so I called the church to check when I didn't hear from him. Mrs. Elmore, his executive secretary, asked me to fax him the call letter and information since he was preaching in a revival service at Shiloh Missionary Baptist Church in Chicago.

At eight in the evening, the phone rang. I heard a deep, distinctive voice say, "This is your pastor."

"Hi, Dr. Sampson, thank you for calling. I hadn't expected to hear from you so soon."

"It appears God has a calling on your life to this church. I announced your opportunity to the congregation at the eight and eleven Sunday morning worship services. The congregation applauded you for a long time. They love you."

"I love you and them too."

"I will look over the documents tomorrow and call you back." He called me the next day.

He said, "Many people at Tab [Tabernacle] contributed to your spiritual formation for such a time as this."

I agreed. Then I said, "I'm concerned about the salary not being as much as I had hoped."

"The low salary reminds me of my first pastorate. I had to pastor on foot for a year, but the Lord blessed us through a family in the church," he said.

I recalled my pastoral leadership class at CIU, taught by Dr. Johnny Miller, our president. He said, "If God has called you somewhere, do not be concerned about the salary." Based on the experience and wisdom of Drs. Sampson and Miller, I decided to adopt this principle then and for the rest of my life in ministry.

Then Dr. Sampson said, "I would like to be your Ananias." His words and tone were loving, and I knew immediately that he was referring to the disciple who ministered to the apostle Paul after his conversion, when he was still called Saul.

Saul had been on his way to Damascus to arrest and imprison Jesus' disciples there. On the way, a flashing light from heaven caused him to fall to the ground, and he heard a voice saying, "Saul, Saul, why do you persecute me?"

Saul asked, "Who are you, Lord?"

The voice answered, "I am Jesus whom you are persecuting."

When Saul arose, he was blind and had to be led to the home of a disciple named Judas.

In the meantime, Jesus appeared in a vision to Ananias and convinced him that Saul was God's chosen instrument to carry the gospel to the gentiles and to his own people, the Jews. Ananias would become a catalyst for Saul's mission. When he laid hands on Saul, his sight was restored, and he was filled with the Holy Spirit. Saul's encounter with Jesus and Ananias was life-changing and life-giving.

When Dr. Sampson said he wanted to serve as my Ananias, I knew it was because he was convinced of the Lord's call on my life to full-time ministry. He saw that I would be an instrument for carrying the gospel in the United States, including at Immanuel Church, and in other countries. Often, just as he used Ananias to help prepare Saul for his ministry, the Lord will use others to support us in different seasons of life and ministry in profound ways. When Dr. Sampson offered to be my Ananias, I knew I had the assurance of his blessing and his commitment to assisting me. He would be the catalyst for my acceptance into the community of faith in Kalamazoo. I felt loved and supported by my pastor.

The next day, I said yes to Immanuel Church's invitation to become their new co-pastor. I expected to move to Kalamazoo in July. Dr. Sampson and the Tabernacle Church family planned to attend my installation service in October.

I would cover a lot of ground in a short period between saying yes to Immanuel Church and moving to Kalamazoo. I proudly walked across the stage to shake President Miller's hand and be awarded my degree from CIU. My family and friends were there. My two sisters, Deborah and Donna, came from Detroit; my aunt Mildred and cousins Cheryl and Shirley drove from Alabama. From Columbia, Pastor Wright of Saint John Baptist Church, two deacons and their wives, a young lady I had mentored, and a deacon's wife and daughter came to celebrate with me. My friend Sara, who was currently in the same program, came. Seminary had been one of the best times in my life, and I received abundant love from my family, friends, staff, and professors, who rejoiced in God's goodness.

After a lovely meal with my family, Cheryl and I returned to my apartment. I told Cheryl about my need to meditate before going to bed, so she left for a while.

I sat at the desk with my eyes closed and waited for the Holy Spirit to give me wisdom and understanding about responding to my new church, community, and denomination. Several themes emerged as areas of commitment and growth, which I would pray for. I wrote each theme on eight-and-a-half-by-eleven-inch paper and taped them on the wall. I paused after each one:

- Love God
- Love one another
- Purify my heart
- Fellowship with God
- Walk as Jesus did

The greatest of these themes is love. First John 4:16 says, "And so we know and rely on the love God has for us. God is love. Whoever lives in love lives in God, and God in them." It anchors my soul to know God's love. His very nature is love. That same love dwells within me. It will never be exhausted; it will never lose its power. There will always be enough love to receive and share. Love is an action. That same love drove Jesus to the cross to die for us. It transcends all racial, cultural, gender, socioeconomic, and other societal barriers. This love is no respecter of persons. It doesn't show favoritism. This love is powerful, and it penetrates the most challenging situations. As Maya Angelou is believed to have said, "Love recognizes no barriers. It jumps hurdles, leaps fences, penetrates walls to arrive at its destination full of hope." Love responds in its own dynamic, intentional way.

God showed me his love through others in tangible ways when I couldn't help myself. I had few financial resources to move from Columbia to Kalamazoo, and I prayed for a financial blessing. I didn't have a reliable car and would also need housing in Kalamazoo. I paid many repair bills for my old red Tempo and gave it to my friend, Denise, who lived on campus but had no transportation. I wasn't going to try driving it for such a long distance.

Several times, "what if" and "maybe" statements came to mind as if I were looking for answers, but then I sought divine guidance. I rested in God's hands and cried out to him in mid-May because I needed money for the move. I remembered God's financial provisions made for my move to Columbia. I waited for the Lord to answer my prayers. My first breakthrough came the next day when my friend Gwen sent me a financial blessing. Then a floodgate opened wide. The monetary gifts kept coming in the mail from Alabama, Michigan, and South Carolina. I thank God for the love poured out to me from those I had known for years and those I had met in Columbia. God put it in their hearts to give.

The Spirit continued to lead me to prepare for my ministry at Immanuel Church by focusing on love. I prayed and asked the Lord to teach me to love and to demonstrate love to others. As I prepared, I sensed a shift to fearlessness in my spirit. I felt that no matter what happened, God loved me, and my heart desired to love and obey him.

One Sunday, not long before I left, I saw my neighbor, Judy, returning from church. She was among the most unique, forgiving people I had ever met, and I asked her, "Judy, what does love look like to you?"

She said, "Love looks like the time my handicapped mother ran water in the bathtub and gave clean clothes to the neighborhood drunk."

I said, "Yes, that's love."

The following Sunday, I went to the Oliver Gospel Mission to say goodbye.

The gospel mission had previously asked me to teach a weekly, daytime Bible lesson there, and Immanuel Church had requested that I take some photos of my ministry with the homeless people there. They would use the photos in their church newsletter. Taking the photos would also give me an opportunity to say goodbye to the people I'd ministered to for six months.

I'd gotten to know one man, Andrew, well. I'd met him when I preached a message at Saint John Baptist Church's Thanksgiving dinner. At the end of my sermon, I invited people to respond to Jesus' call to accept his love and forgiveness. Four homeless men and one woman came to the front of the fellowship hall. I wrote their names on a piece of paper, and I visited the Oliver Gospel Mission the following week to invite them to Saint John's worship service and discipleship class.

Andrew was the only one I made a connection with. We agreed I would pick him up, take him to the service, and afterward, we would go to the Richland Memorial Hospital for a good, affordable meal in the cafeteria. I listened to how he had fallen into hard times and was saddened to hear the circumstances that had broken up his family.

Andrew was always clean, kind, and grateful. He wouldn't tell me where he slept during the night, but he impressed me as someone who was streetwise. I made no assumptions, nor did I ask why he wouldn't tell me. I would drive on if I didn't see Andrew waiting for me on our designated street corner.

Now, That's Love

By the time I was ready to leave Columbia, although I continued to see Andrew and some of the other clients at the gospel mission, Andrew had stopped attending our church's worship services. The day I went to take our pictures, I told the clients about my opportunity to be part of a pastoral team at Immanuel Church in Kalamazoo, Michigan.

Andrew stood and said, "All right, everybody, I want you to help her."

We took several lovely pictures. It was close to dinner time, and the clients got in line to be served. Andrew and I talked for a long time that day. Then he asked, "How are you getting back to Detroit?" It seemed so unusual for a homeless person to be concerned about me. He spoke to me as a friend would.

I said, "I don't know right now. God will lead me one step at a time."

"Will you allow me to walk you to your car?"

"Yes, thank you." I told everyone inside goodbye.

When we got to my car, I said to Andrew, "I believe God has something better planned for you." He smiled.

I extended my hand to shake Andrew's hand, but he withdrew his hand, so we hugged goodbye. Then he said, "I also want to shake your hand."

I extended my hand again, not realizing what he was about to do. He placed a wrinkled bill in my hand. When he had left and I got into the car, I looked in my hand and saw he'd given me a well-circulated five-dollar bill. The Spirit put in my heart and mind the words, "Now, that's love." Tears flowed. I've continued to pray for Andrew for years, asking that God would reunite him with his wife and family. I hope God has answered those prayers.

I believe Andrew and the clients at the Oliver Gospel Mission saw God's light shining in me. Hagberg and Guelich, in *The Critical Journey*, introduce the readers to stage six—"The Life of Love." When others see God's light reflecting through our lives, and they give God the glory, we are living a life of love. If they aren't aware of who is responsible for the light shining from us, we acknowledge God as the source. Life is no longer about us but about being invested in God's purpose for our lives. Our obedience is motivated by a reciprocal love relationship between God and his creation. The love we show is life-giving to others, and they enjoy being around us. We are at peace with God and self.[1]

The week after my visit to the gospel mission, I began searching for a used car in the classified section of the newspaper, and I found an

---

1. Hagberg and Guelich, *Critical Journey*, 152–53.

Oldsmobile Achieva at the Dick Smith Nissan dealership. I liked its appearance and performance. When I called the credit union that I had been a member of since I was eighteen, I could not get an auto loan because I had not been employed for at least ninety days. Dick Smith Nissan agreed to finance my car at a higher interest rate without a cosigner because I had a good credit rating. I now had a car and insurance without any money transactions. After ninety days, I refinanced the car at my credit union at a lower rate.

A few days later, while walking in the seminary's courtyard, I crossed paths with Beverly from the administration office. She was the person who had invited me to the celebration for the first woman chaplain in the Air Force. And it was my connection there with Chaplain Eddie Walters that led me to Immanuel Church's job opening.

Beverly asked, "So, Denise, what have you decided to do, now that you've graduated?"

"I've accepted a co-pastor position at Immanuel Christian Reformed Church in Kalamazoo, Michigan."

"What!" She laughed softly. "You're going to be like Daniel in the lion's den."

I had no idea what she meant, but Beverly was familiar with southwest Michigan and had previously been involved with the Dunamis Project, a charismatic Presbyterian-Reformed ministry that emphasized the work of the Holy Spirit and the use of spiritual gifts. The project has been engaged for years with various Reformed denominations.

Beverly's words had piqued my curiosity about what God had planned for me and Immanuel Church. I didn't think to ask her why she said these words about me being like Daniel in the lion's den; however, I knew God was speaking to me, and I would not forget. Only God knew what I would encounter.

Beverly and I hugged goodbye, and she wished me well. Later, I read several chapters of the book of Daniel in the Bible. I saw that Daniel had been practicing a spiritual prayer discipline shortly before being thrown into the lion's den. I, too, had cultivated a strong prayer life, and I wondered again what the connection might be.

Whatever I was destined to go through, I knew I would not be alone. I was at peace because I remembered God had his hand on me. He was not going to allow my feet to slip. I also knew Dr. Sampson would be there for me. I was certain it was God's will for me to serve at Immanuel CRC. I prayed that whatever I was about to encounter, I would stand firm in ways that glorified God.

After some of the conversations I'd had as a candidate at Immanuel, I did have a sense that there was something going on under the surface. If I was told about any concerns, I didn't listen well. In my journal, regarding this feeling, I wrote, "Privileges and burdens," but I didn't think at the time about what it meant. It wasn't until I had been at Immanuel for at least four months that it came to me that Immanuel Church and the Christian Reformed denomination would be a place of both privileges and burdens. As I began to reflect on those words, I saw an image of two hands balancing privileges and burdens. The privileges outweighed the burdens, although not necessarily in a tangible way. They weren't based on my merit but on God's grace. The burdens resulted when I allowed myself to be weighed down or let my circumstances rock my world.

When I came to terms with the reality of privileges and burdens, I realized that, like some other new seminary graduates, I hadn't had a realistic understanding of the nature of the church. The church is made up of broken people. God has called the church to live in this world but not to take on the ways of the world. Even within the church we fall short of God's glory when, although we are the body of Christ, we yield to the temptations of the flesh and act out of a lack of awareness of the forces of evil working against us.

Privileges and burdens are inherent characteristics of being followers of Jesus Christ no matter where we serve. We experience both. One person's privilege might be perceived as a burden to someone else and vice versa. Ministry is not all mountains or valleys; it's both. It has highs and lows, like marriages and other relationships. Often, when new pastors see this, their response is to want to leave. Dr. Sampson often said, "Don't leave by the nearest exit." God would teach me to thrive even in adversity.

After saying goodbye to my CIU and church families, it was time to say goodbye to one of my closest friends, my "big sister" in Columbia—Judy. It was a bittersweet moment when we hugged. Judy gave the best hugs.

I left Columbia in my new car at eight o'clock in the morning. On the journey home, I stopped to fill the gas tank, go to the restroom, and get an Arby's roast beef sandwich. And once I stopped to take a power nap for twenty minutes. I got weary between Lima, Ohio, and Detroit. I had a cousin in Lima, but I wanted to go home. On the last stretch of my drive, I felt numb and couldn't see straight. I was so close to Detroit when I missed my exit because the interstate was under construction. I ended up in an area known for gang activity. At one point, I saw several police cars with flashing lights surrounding a car. I thank God the only incident was getting lost for a few moments. I got back on track and arrived at my parents' house at twelve forty-five in the morning. Knowing my parents, they had been praying for my safe arrival.

As I moved to another chapter in my journey, I imagined an auditorium filled with chosen people assigned to accomplish God's plan during each episode in my life. I could see them at the entrance, on the main floor, in the center, on the left and right stages, in the balcony, and at the exit. God was directing the story. All the players received cues from the Holy Spirit to execute God's story of my life.

The gospel songwriter tells the greatest love story in the song "No Greater Love" that I kept hearing as I prepared for my ministry at Immanuel. It told the story of Jesus going to Calvary to save us, of his dying on the cross with his arms stretched wide, of his rising again. All punctuated throughout with the line, "That's love, that's love." What God accomplished by sending his Son had made me want to follow Jesus anywhere. His love had healed me; it propelled me to love others.

STONE OF REMEMBRANCE: LOVE

Remembering that God so often used others to accomplish his purposes for my life has carried me through many challenging times and kept me focused on the mission. I have never felt or thought I wasn't loved by God and those he places in my life to support me. God is love. God's love radiates from us to others. "See what great love the Father has lavished on us, that we should be called children of God! And that is what we are!" (1 John 3:1).

REFLECTION QUESTIONS

What is your story of who helped nurture, affirm, and support you for God's assignment? What effect does remembering your critical moment have on you? What was God's role? What did you learn about him? In what ways have you shared your God story with others? What is your stone of remembrance?

11

A Glimpse of a Heavenly Vision

> After this I looked, and there before me was a great multitude that no one could count, from every nation, tribe, people, and language, standing before the throne and before the Lamb. They were wearing white robes and were holding palm branches in their hands. —Rev 7:9

I HAD WAITED A long time for this moment, and then things started to move quickly. Members from Immanuel Church were at my new apartment when my nephews arrived in a large moving truck. I pointed to where I wanted things, and we had fun while we worked.

I felt blessed with a new church, my pastoral position, the community, and the denomination I would be getting to know. I was grateful. However, I was quickly saddened to hear that two white couples had left the church. One pair didn't believe God called women to be pastors, and I didn't know why the other couple left.

As a longtime member of the Baptist tradition, I looked forward to learning more about the Reformed faith traditions. One of my first opportunities came with an early official business meeting of pastors, elders, and deacons from twenty-three CRC churches in Indiana and Michigan. Combined, these churches are called a "classis"—in this case, Classis Kalamazoo. I will never forget that experience, which was both welcoming and, as it progressed, shocking.

In the narthex of our hosting church, I passed several large portraits of earlier pastors. Someone should have told them to smile; their faces looked stone-cold and emotionless. If these men were here right now, would they be happy to see me—a black woman pastor—joining their denomination? I wondered. Mentally I said, "Well, here I am by God's grace!"

When I passed the kitchen, I saw women preparing lunch, and as I entered the sanctuary, I saw the backs of the heads of white men. Two couples, Dorothy and Dale Van Hamersveld and Ruth and Nelson Gritter, came over to meet and welcome me. They wanted to be sure to connect with me because of their important work in the denomination. They had been pioneers on the Committee for Women in the CRC, organized formally after a 1975 decision by Synod to not open offices in the church to women. Synod is an annual meeting where important decisions are made on behalf of the denomination. Those who advocated for women in office made a major step forward in 1995 when Synod voted to allow individual churches to make independent decisions about women holding office.[1] This decision still operates in the CRC today.

Later, whenever the Van Hamersvelds and Gritters were present, they were quick to connect with me every time I came to a classis meeting, always making sure I felt welcome.

At my first classis meeting, the chairperson said to Mark, "Denise should be ready directly after lunch to introduce herself, before we enter the second half of the business portion of our meeting."

After lunch, Mark made a few preliminary comments about our church and how we planned to work together in our ministry. He said he and Immanuel Church were grateful to have me on board.

I placed one foot before the other as I walked from my seat to the podium. I paused as I stood center stage. Stillness filled the room. All eyes were fixed on me. With confidence and a smile, I said, "Praise the Lord! This is the day the Lord has made; let us rejoice and be glad in it. I am happy to accept the call as co-pastor of Immanuel Christian Reformed Church! I am a yielded vessel looking forward to serving God's people. I know God has called me to the Christian Reformed Church, and I am honored to be here." I shared that I grew up in Detroit and attended Columbia International University's seminary. I was blessed by hearty applause after my last word. I confidently returned to my seat.

I wasn't ready for what came next.

Someone raised the question of whether women—in my case, a woman pastor—should be allowed to serve a church in this classis. My heart

---

1. Christian Reformed Church, "Women in Ecclesiastical Office," paras. 5–6.

was pierced every time I heard my name mentioned in ways that were far from affirming. I felt awkward, even though some in the group were clearly welcoming me. I felt myself fading into the background, wondering why they were having this discussion in my presence. I thought, "Wow, is this really happening?"

Then it occurred to me that none of what I was experiencing in Classis Kalamazoo was a surprise to God. I knew the council and congregation of Immanuel, as part of Classis Kalamazoo, were ready for me. In my heart, I knew God had gone before me to prepare the way, whatever that might mean. I knew that I was following God's will for my life.

Classis Kalamazoo as a whole entity wasn't ready for an African American woman pastor, or any woman pastor. I would be the only woman clergy member ordained and serving in a pastoral role there, but I was not ordained in the CRC. I don't think this classis had talked beforehand about how to handle it if a woman pastor was called to one of their churches. They talked as if I weren't in the room with them. I thought about my friend Beverly's prophetic word about Daniel in the lion's den when I told her I had accepted a position on a pastoral team in the CRC, a denomination she was familiar with. I also recalled a wise word from a female associate pastor in a United Methodist Church in Columbia. She had said, "Stay focused on God's mission." I needed to be aware of the lions but not let anything distract me from God's mission.

A month later, I was installed as Immanuel CRC's co-pastor. There was never an installation service like mine in Classis Kalamazoo, then or later. God used it to prepare the way for the new kid on the block. Dr. Sampson and the Tabernacle Missionary Baptist Church family came out in full force. They arrived in separate cars and a large, chartered bus from Detroit and included the Choraleer Gospel Choir under the directorship of Gregory Adams. My parents, family, and friends came from Michigan and Ohio. My CIU friends, Reverends Yvonne Frederick and Sara Smith, came from Columbia. The mayor of Kalamazoo, Robert Jones, and representatives of nonprofit and civic organizations came, including Dr. Charles Warfield, president of the Metropolitan Kalamazoo Branch of the NAACP. Pastor J. Louis Felton, president of the Northside Ministerial Alliance, and members of the greater Kalamazoo churches filled the house. Four pastors from Classis Kalamazoo came, and two were on the program. I was deeply honored to receive all this support.

Rev. Ben Becksvoort, the CRC Great Lakes Regional Leader, and Rev. Al Mulder came from the CRC Home Missions office in Grand Rapids. By the time of my installation, I had gotten to know both of them well because a couple of months earlier, Ben had asked me to serve on the Home Missions Anti-Racism Committee on which Al Mulder served. They were supportive of my calling and decision to join the CRC.

Reverend Mulder walked arm-in-arm with me down the aisle to my front-row seat, draped in purple cloth, while the outstanding Immanuel worship team and lead vocalist, David Veenstra, sang "Prepare Ye the Way of the Lord." A harpist, Ben Brown, who was a former member of Immanuel from years ago, offered a lovely solo. Pastor Mark and my new church family showed up and supported me thoroughly. They had asked for my input in planning the celebration to ensure it was what I wanted. Immanuel's worship team was the best. Dr. Sampson's message was titled "There's a Fever in the House," from Luke 4:38–40, when Jesus and the disciples stopped at Peter's house and found his mother-in-law with a high fever. The disciples asked Jesus to help her, and he bent over her and rebuked the fever. She got up from the bed and waited on them. I understood the message as a reminder of the house I was entering, a new denomination. *It's going to be hot. Not everyone agrees that you belong here.* He said, "God above all things; no matter what happens to you, obey God." This was not an assignment orchestrated by any person; this was God's doing. My pastor preached with conviction and passion! He knew I was entering unfamiliar territory and places where a black woman pastor had not gone before in this community. Some colleagues had said, "You are shattering stained-glass ceilings." I had thought about the experiences God had used to prepare me for this season of transition, like my dream of his glorious diverse kingdom.

The ecumenical service was a celebration of heaven here on earth, demonstrating the diversity and unity of God's kingdom. Afro–Puerto Rican, African American, and Caucasian pastors filled the small pulpit area on closely placed seats. It was a lovely sight to witness. At the end, choir director Greg invited us to stand to sing the uplifting, worshipful song "Total Praise," by gospel artist Richard Smallwood. My entry into Kalamazoo resounded with welcome, and a significant reason was that Dr. Sampson was my Ananias; he blessed me and opened the door for me as a woman pastor in Kalamazoo. Reverend Becksvoort's support paved the way for me to connect with the broader CRC community. I was prayed over and esteemed by my brothers and sisters in Christ. I had allies in both Kalamazoo and Grand Rapids, the denomination's headquarters.

A month later, on the front page of the religion section in the *Kalamazoo Gazette*, a tall headline read, "Diversity in the Pulpit." I was thrilled about Immanuel's vision and the denomination's stance on what we then called "dismantling racism." Mark had said we would work well together because we had different strengths but a singular vision—a diverse church. I agreed with what Rev. Kenneth Baker, now retired pastor of Third Christian Reformed Church in Kalamazoo, said in writer Dave Person's article, "She [Denise] brings a diversity that helps us to better reflect on what the church should be, and what the church is intended to be in terms of an entity that is gathered from all peoples." Person wrote, "There were no indications early in Posie's life that she would break racial and gender barriers in the Christian Reformed's Classis Kalamazoo."[2]

The *Gazette* article opened the door for a double blessing. The church received a call from Ben Boersma, the owner of Mall City Containers, a manufacturer of corrugated boxes, located about a mile and a half from the church. Ben wanted me to consider working part time as an industrial chaplain for his company. I visited him to learn more, and we were both pleased with the opportunity, expectations, and salary. There was an extra bonus when Ben and I sat in his office to talk about the Lord and the ministry in the factory. I served at Mall City for five years, and I knew when it was time for me to resign. Ben and his wife, Cleo, prayed for me and followed my journey even after I left. I will not forget them.

Immanuel Church and I had a lot to be thankful for. I was ready and set to go, and the church was too. I couldn't know everything, but within a few months, I noticed things were not as I had imagined. As time went on, after the honeymoon, I learned about the Immanuel members' stories, history, and their life together. I observed that many were still grieving the unexpected departure of their previous pastor who had led them in their heyday, prior to Mark's tenure. I began to realize that the church might not be ready to reach out to the community. I kept my eyes, ears, and heart open.

As a pastoral team, Mark and I sometimes walked the neighborhood during the week to meet people on the streets or to knock on doors. We took part weekly in the Northside Ministerial Alliance (NMA), a prominent ecumenical organization for clergy and leaders working collaboratively for

---

2. Person, "Diversity in the Pulpit," D1.

the betterment of the community. This was a wonderful body, especially for pastors' renewal through the preached word and gospel singing. It was good for support and much-needed fellowship. I quickly became connected with this group, which opened doors to serving a broader community. Dr. J. Louis Felton, president of NMA and the pastor of Galilee Baptist Church, and Pastor Mark and Immanuel had formed a close relationship over the years. Earlier, the two churches had become a blessing to each other. They had prayed for the new co-pastor.

Mark and I knew that becoming a racially diverse church would require intentionality and going beyond the church walls, as well as ministering to current members' needs. It would take a balancing act. I envisioned Immanuel Church's neighborhood as a mission field for community development, including an after-school tutorial program. Mark and I were on the same page with this vision. However, I was unsettled about whether Immanuel should focus on being a racially diverse church. The church makeup was 90 percent Caucasian, 8 percent African American, and 2 percent Cuban, from various socioeconomic statuses, professions, and parts of the city. Most members, including myself, didn't live within a mile of the church. Some people think this is important; however, I learned there must be a natural, cultural, and Holy Spirit connection between the church and its neighbors.

A conflict arose among some members of Immanuel. Immanuel's council sought the help of Pastor-Church Relations (now Thrive Ministries), from the denominational headquarters, to lead the congregation through a conflict resolution process. It was an intense and painful time at Immanuel for everyone except those members who had no inkling about the conflict. It was disappointing for me as Immanuel's new pastor, but I knew that I wasn't the reason for the conflict.

During this time, I observed what is referred to as "standing on the balcony," also called "practicing self-differentiation." Edwin H. Friedman offers a good description of self-differentiation in his book *A Failure of Nerve*. He says it happens when someone "has clarity about his or her own life goals, and, therefore, . . . is less likely to become lost in the anxious emotional processes swirling about . . . while still remaining connected."[3] Friedman captures how I coped and connected, especially during this time. My posture kept me from being enmeshed in an anxious system. I did not

---

3. Friedman, *Failure of Nerve*, 14.

know at the time what this was called, but I knew it was the right thing for me to do.

The mediation process of listening circles and one-on-one conversations lasted for months. Sometimes, I was around for them, and at other times, I wasn't. I saw the messy stuff below the iceberg, but I tried not to let anything get between our pastor-congregation relationship.

I don't know who decided it at the end of this part of the journey, but Pastor Mark and Immanuel would sever their relationship. I had become friends with Mark and his wife, Patricia, and we are still friends today. My heart was broken. I hadn't intended to be the sole pastor, especially in my first call and in a denomination I didn't know well.

When I knew what was happening, I contacted Rev. Vern Luchies, the first full-time pastor of Immanuel, and asked to visit him. Reverend Luchies greeted me as I entered the enclosed porch of their home, located within minutes of Immanuel Church. The seventy-something, white-haired retired pastor waited to discuss the purpose of my visit until his wife sat by his side. I didn't know it at the time, but he was practicing what is referred to as the "Billy Graham Rule." It meant that evangelical men would not spend time alone with women other than their wives—a way of setting boundaries. After telling him about Immanuel's latest happenings, I said, "I didn't come here to pastor alone."

Reverend Luchies said, "Sometimes God works in mysterious ways. You can do it with the Lord's help." I am sure he had thought about the Lord's provisions for Immanuel for forty-five years.

I said, "Yes, I know."

He talked briefly about Immanuel's resilience, then closed in prayer. I was grateful for the visit and to have hope for the future.

I missed Mark. Going forward, I felt both excitement and trepidation, but I tried to stay focused on God's mission. I attended the Classis Kalamazoo meetings alone, although many of the pastors reached out to me in various ways.

One beautiful sunny day, I was walking through the neighborhood when I saw an elderly African American gentleman wearing a black suit with a white shirt and tie. I wondered where he was going dressed so nicely on a weekday.

I said, "Hello, sir."

He said, "Hello. How are you on this fine day?"

"My name is Denise Posie. I'm doing fine. I am the new pastor at the church on the corner, Immanuel Christian Reformed Church."

He gave me his name and introduced himself as an elder in the Church of God in Christ (COGIC) denomination. What he said next surprised me, and I've always remembered it.

"Baby, you must have the skin of a rhinoceros." I laughed, but he was serious. Having the skin of a rhinoceros would offer protection from anyone or anything that might attack me or keep me from flourishing. What frightening images for starting a new ministry, lion's den and rhinoceros, but I remembered the empowering words of the Lord—that my feet would not slip and that his hand was on me.

When Classis Kalamazoo approached me to become an ordained minister in the CRC within my first year and also thereafter, I prayed diligently, but I did not sense the Spirit's leading. I contacted my academic advisor at CIU to discuss my dilemma. He gave me godly counsel and prayed for me to remain faithful to God's call and guidance. I did, with God's help.

STONE OF REMEMBRANCE: DIVERSITY

A glimpse of God's heavenly vision is embedded in my memory. Through the Spirit's work, it keeps me at the cross, where it is level for all peoples. God's love for diversity influences how I treat and minister to others (1 Cor 12:12–27).

REFLECTION QUESTIONS

What characteristic or gift has God given you and has it become an integral part of who you are and how you engage with others? When did you first notice it and how? How are others affected by it? What is your stone of remembrance?

12

Was It Worth It?

> Returning back for grace, healing, and closure is a fascinating practice.
> —Freida Watson

Two years after my installation, any trepidation I had was put to rest when I had the privilege to join a delegation on a trip to New York City that included a meeting with the first African American evangelist and Minister of the Word in the Christian Reformed denomination, Rev. Dr. Eugene Callender. In the 1950s, he reached many lost souls, helped start a drug addiction treatment center, dealt with landlords who charged tenants too much rent, and built a solid inner-city outreach ministry in Harlem. He helped extend the reach of the Christian Reformed Home Missions and the *Back to God Hour* (the CRC's radio ministry) into the African American community. Callender faithfully served the Mid-Harlem Community Parish until he abruptly left the CRC in 1959.[1]

During our visit, we introduced ourselves.

I said, "I am the pastor of Immanuel CRC, and I live in Kalamazoo."

Dr. Callender smiled and said, "I will be in Kalamazoo soon. I am a fellow of the Fetzer Institute."

I was familiar with the Fetzer Institute, which fosters love and unity of humans as one family in the world and values everyone as having a purpose to fulfill.

---

1. Parker, "CRC's First Black Pastor," 8.

"I want you to be our guest preacher on the Sunday you're in town," I told him.

"Absolutely. I would love to come." He expressed how proud he was that I was called to pastor a Christian Reformed Church. I felt his love and respect for me. I can only imagine how he felt after being away from the CRC for many years. He was meeting a delegation of ten African American pastors, one of whom was a woman pastor. God's hand was in this visit led by Dr. Bob Price, our Home Missions ethnic leader, who provided us with some historical context. Sometimes, when someone leaves a church, denomination, or institution, the departure is often hushed, as if the person never existed.

I was surprised later, when the *Kalamazoo Gazette* contacted me about writing a feature on Callender after seeing the event I had listed in the *Gazette*'s church happenings column. Their interest was that he had been asked to leave the Christian Reformed denomination after his divorce. He had yet to return to speak under the auspices of our denomination, prior to this invitation. I agreed to having the article written.

The *Gazette*'s story, "A Blessing in Disguise," highlighted the fact that the first black CRC pastor had been invited to speak for the first time within the denomination that had exiled him. Callender was quoted as saying that while there were bitter feelings at his departure, he had long since realized that leaving the CRC was a blessing in disguise. He said the move allowed him to branch out in his work, eventually becoming pastor of the largest Presbyterian church in New York City and serving as an advisor to five presidents.[2]

I received several phone calls when his forthcoming visit was made public. One call was from the renowned Reverend Dr. Lewis Smedes, an author, theologian, and longtime friend of Dr. Callender's. I gave him Dr. Callender's phone number. I was stunned that Dr. Smedes had already known about our ministry at Immanuel through Christian Reformed publications. He commended me for serving in our denomination as an African American woman.

Rev. Duane VanderBrug emailed me to praise God for how much Dr. Callender means to him and his wife, Adele. God had blessed them to have been shaped in urban ministry by Dr. Callender and his ministry. It warmed my heart to read, "This Sunday, you will have a front-row seat in

---

2. Meehan, "Blessing in Disguise," D1.

the healing that God is bringing to the church!" His words caused calmness to rise up in my heart.

One day, while I was in the church office, the phone rang. It was one of my colleagues in the CRC. I was surprised.

He said, "Denise, I want to talk to you about Dr. Callender's visit."

I said, "Okay."

"Will you meet me halfway between here and Kalamazoo?"

"Yes." We met about forty-five minutes later. We got coffee, and he began talking about the nature of his call.

I said, "So, what's up?"

"Do you know what you are doing by inviting Dr. Callender back to the CRC as a guest preacher? He was released as a pastor due to his divorce. You don't know what you're doing."

"But I need him to return to where his story began, to encourage and inspire many like me. He was a trailblazer! The Spirit led me to invite him back."

He nodded.

"I hope you're right." We talked briefly, hugged, and then parted ways. I was surprised by his concern because he is a person of color, so I thought he would have understood. I appreciated his concern though.

Dr. Callender came back after over forty years!

His visit became quite a reunion. On Sunday morning, May 21, 2001, the church was packed. This represented another ecumenical event. The Kalamazoo Christian High School Gospel Choir sang. Jason Veenstra, a member of Immanuel, was in the choir. The *Banner*, the CRC's magazine, covered the occasion. The Reverend Peter Borgdorff, executive director of ministries for the CRC, was quoted at that time saying, "Posie is herself a trailblazer as one of the first (of only two) African American women to pastor a Christian Reformed church, and her ministry also focuses on racial and social outreach. Callender helped to begin the kind of urban ministry in the CRC that Posie is now doing in Kalamazoo."[3]

The colleague who had called me out about inviting Callender came to the celebration, after all. Later he said that he was glad I had invited Dr. Callender. We didn't know then the full impact of Dr. Callender's visit, but God was up to something good. His hand was clearly working things out for God's glory.

---

3. Parker, "CRC's First Black Pastor," 8.

When I met Dr. Callender in New York, I had asked him, "Was it worth it?" I wanted to know if being part of the Christian Reformed denomination was a meaningful and worthwhile experience. He understood what I meant. We had something in common.

Dr. Callender paused to reflect on his life and career. "Yes," he answered.

His response to the same question upon visiting Immanuel was captured by Jennifer Parker in the *Banner*. She wrote, "One of the reasons Posie wanted so much to meet Callender was to ask him, looking back, how he feels about his career and the outcome of his association with the CRC. 'I wanted to ask him this question *again*,' Posie said: Was it worth it?"

Parker continued, "But Callender bears no grudges, only gratitude. 'I am deeply grateful to the CRC for giving birth to my ministry,' he said. Whatever bitterness he might have felt at the time, Callender realizes now that his departure from the CRC was a springboard that allowed him to take his ministry in new directions and to give his social justice ministry a much larger scope."[4]

It was clear that Dr. Callender had all the while been fulfilling God's call, and his words touched the core of my soul and gave me the confidence to keep on. I would leave the results to God. He is the only One who knows the end of the story.

Chris Meehan of the *Gazette* expressed my sentiment. "As one of the first African American women to pastor a CRC church, she has dedicated herself to an urban ministry that combines the message of the Gospel with social and racial outreach."[5]

Another life-giving experience happened in 2007 when I attended Courage to Lead, a retreat program for clergy and congregational leaders held at the Fetzer Institute in Kalamazoo, along with three local clergy and other leaders/clergy in the United States. Courage to Lead was part of the Center for Courage and Renewal, founded by Parker J. Palmer and Marcy Jackson. Palmer is a Quaker, writer, speaker, and activist.

We met each quarter of the year in large, small, and individual sessions for reflection. In my small group circle of trust, in the winter season, I explored whether it was time for me to leave Immanuel. I felt torn. Perhaps you are aware of the seven-year itch—when pastors are trying to determine whether to stay or go because something needs to change. According to

---

4. Parker, "CRC's First Black Pastor," 9.
5. Meehan, "Blessing in Disguise," D1.

Was It Worth It?

Dave Odom, executive director of leadership at Duke University, it is easier to see when we look back that the uneasiness we experience at the seven-year mark is normal.[6] I didn't realize it at the time, but it stood true for my previous three jobs in the corporate and private sectors.

My circle of trust colleagues supported me by asking open-ended questions without judging, trying to fix or resolve my situation. I wondered if my time was coming close to an end because of what I was experiencing—difficulty preparing sermons, having no administrative support in the office after years support, and the challenges of being a single pastor. It was a dry season. One of those challenges was that I hadn't been creating natural boundaries for a more balanced life, including being able to visit my Detroit family and friends.

For example, I still regret preaching one Sunday instead of going to see my mother in the hospital in Detroit. I wish I had told Immanuel's elders I had to visit Detroit to see my mother. Although it would have been especially short notice for a preacher, two members of the congregation were ordained Christian Reformed clergy and could have stepped in. Instead, I called the hospital to ask for a chaplain to check on my mother, pray for her, and call back and leave a message. I explained my situation. I told Chaplain Mary that I needed a message from her by the end of our service. She gave me her word. Chaplain Mary left a message that my mother was resting well, and she had prayed with her the Jesus Prayer, which was, "Lord Jesus Christ, Son of God, have mercy." I was grateful for her service and report. A warm human connection lifts the spirit. I left to go to Detroit after morning worship.

A visit to the hospital that morning would have been better. There's always one more need in church ministry, one more person to reach out to. Sometimes, it takes effort to pull away from something you love doing.

It was good for me to pull away from my regular schedule to attend the Courage to Lead retreat. It opened my eyes and heart to a new way of understanding my call and assignment. Parker Palmer visited our last session to introduce a concept called standing in the tragic gap. Palmer says, "*By 'the tragic gap' I mean the gap between what is and what could and should be, the gap between the reality of a given situation and an alternative reality we know to be possible because we have experienced it.*"[7]

---

6. Odom, "Seven Year Itch."
7. Palmer, "Broken-Open Heart," 8; emphasis in original.

Through my experience at Immanuel, I resonated with standing in the tragic gap as it relates to becoming a multiracial church. It was a difficult place and a rough road to travel. The complexity of my cultural and theological differences and the history of the Dutch people in southwest Michigan regarding racism were major factors that I and Immanuel did not consider when I came to the church and the Christian Reformed denomination. My gender may have contributed as well.

Palmer invited us to consider writing our story of standing in the tragic gap. The assignment included a four-day retreat in Valparaiso, Indiana, following the one-year Courage to Lead retreat. I was one of four pastors in our group whose stories were featured in the *Weavings Journal*'s quarterly issue, which was dedicated to Parker Palmer's concept of standing in the tragic gap. It was an incredible experience and my first time collaborating with a professional editor. My piece was titled "Rising with New Courage and New Hope," and I wrote about an explosive council meeting in which I shared a proposal for a summer theater camp for kids from within and outside the church. I thought my proposal had been unjustly scrutinized.

I was hurt and angry, though I tried to keep an open heart. I was a bottom-line person, but not everyone was like me; some people needed more than basic information. My approach had been to simply look for what needed to happen to get the ball rolling. I met the council's concerns and their request to invite the professional theater team, with which we would contract, to join us and answer the council's questions. It ended with everyone being satisfied. We were able to move forward with the Summer Stages Theater Camp for four successful, consecutive summers, with grants from a local foundation.[8]

Something crucial I learned from that experience was that as I become clearer about who I am, I am better able to understand others; I become more open to God's new creation for me, in me, through me, and around me. I am assured of his grace to hold the tension. When I am overwhelmed, God enables me to rise, once again, with new courage and new hope—blessings from God for me and for others. This has happened over and over since I've been an ordained minister.

Standing in the tragic gap is as relevant today as it was then. I embraced this way of living into my calling in 2008; Palmer gave me the language to understand my calling and experiences. My engagement with this concept is one of the major reasons I did not prematurely leave Immanuel Church.

---

8. Posie, "Rising with New Courage," 40.

God brought our church through some troubled waters, and he was still with us. We were bearing fruit internally and externally. No matter what the circumstances are, I can and am determined to stand in the tragic gap.

My heart has remained open to being used as God's vessel to serve in the Christian Reformed denomination. I've never felt like I fully fitted in culturally and theologically, but I always remembered that my calling to serve was from God. I was grateful for two African American brothers: Dr. Bob Price of Chicago, then the ethnic leader in Home Missions, and Dr. Reggie Smith, former pastor of Roosevelt Park CRC in Grand Rapids. They enlightened me about the Dutch culture and the denomination upon my arrival at Immanuel and reminded me of who I am and that I was not alone.

For decades, wherever God opened a door for ministry, I tried to serve courageously and faithfully. My calling expanded as I joined God in building his kingdom in congregations in the United States and Canada, as a congregational consultant, the codirector of the Reformed Leadership Initiative (a Reformed Church of America and CRC collaboration), and the director of leadership diversity, serving women clergy and diverse leaders, including the Black and Reformed Leadership Network. Each position and opportunity have come with unique risks, challenges, and rewards.

Outside of the denomination, I served with several nonprofit community organizations and became the first and only woman president of the Northside Ministerial Alliance after Dr. J. Louis Felton, the former president, accepted a call in another state in 2010.

In 2024, while writing this chapter, I was gripped by unexpected and unresolved feelings regarding that first Classis Kalamazoo meeting long ago. I was led by the Spirit to reach out to this classis and get permission to share my painful story. I appreciated a phone call from Rev. Mike Koetje, pastor of Westwood Christian Reformed Church and chair of the Classical Interim Team, regarding my request. He was concerned, curious, and pastoral in his response. He asked, "What would you like to share and why now?"

"I would like three to five minutes to say who I am, why I came to the CRC, and why I am here now. I am writing a spiritual memoir, and I couldn't continue because I felt the pain of my first meeting with Classis Kalamazoo. It is not my intent to cast any blame or shame. I know there has been a change in leadership now anyway."

"Yes, we would like for you to come." He expressed sadness and concern about my experience. Mike closed our conversation in a heartfelt prayer.

I went to the meeting to share for five minutes about my disappointment as a new pastor in Kalamazoo with what I perceived was a lack of acceptance. I had endured as an African American woman in the clergy when I came to that first meeting. Poet David Whyte wrote a poem called "The Journey" after a friend had gone through a difficult time.[9] Similar to the geese he mentions in the poem, I had to return to the light to receive something new written in my heart. In returning, the words, "I'm not leaving, but I'm arriving" resonate with my arrival at a new juncture in my life, a place of peace with God, myself, Classis Kalamazoo, and the CRC. When there is interpersonal conflict, I tend to address it within a short period. In this case, however, the conflict was theological and institutional in nature, and I believe that is why I didn't meet with classis to discuss the experience years ago. It would be like hitting my head against a wall. However, I was ready to write this chapter of my life because there was something for all of us to learn.

To my surprise, the president that night was Rev. Maria Bowater, a Minister of the Word and Sacrament and executive pastor of RedArrow Ministries in Paw Paw, Michigan. I had been her vocational group leader at Calvin Theological Seminary. She joined me at the lectern to pray and gave me a hearty hug. Everyone was invited for refreshments downstairs afterward. Several men and women approached me with apologies and warm thoughts. It was a grace-filled visit. I'm glad I was led to return.

Fortunately, I wasn't inhibited to love myself and minister to others. I ministered from a position of grace as a "wounded healer." My heart was opened to authentically minister to individuals in their suffering because of my own past experiences. Through the power of the Spirit working in and through me, individuals found hope, healing, and life. I wasn't a victim. Author of *The Wounded Healer*, Henri J. M. Nouwen says, "Like Jesus he [the wounded healer] who proclaims liberation is called not only to care for his own wounds and the wounds of others, but also to make his wounds into a major source of his healing power."[10]

---

9. Whyte, "Journey."
10. Nouwen, *Wounded Healer*, 82–83.

Was It Worth It?

I, too, can say, like Dr. Callender, that Immanuel Church was God's springboard for new opportunities and blessings to serve in the Christian Reformed Church and beyond. I, too, am grateful.

Nothing was more apparent to me than God's call, strength, love, power, and anointing for each assignment. In *The Critical Journey*, Hagberg and Guelich's words ring true for me: "God promises to use our weakness to do God's work. We can respond in ways that utterly astound others, because we are not operating on our own power or energy anymore. We are God's."[11] I had no doubt about the sustainability of the healing power of God. I never would have made it.

My twenty years of service in the Christian Reformed denomination were challenging at times, but it has been worth it. It has been a bittersweet journey, and such is life. If God were to ask me, "Denise, if you could do it all over again, would you still say yes?" My answer would be yes. I have learned that there is a path that some people must take, and no matter how much others want them to take a different path, it won't happen if they are following God's will. I was following his will, and I would do it again. The journey was costly at times, but I have also met, served with, and grown to love wonderful, good people. I gained some friends, and I lost some. "At Stage Six, 'The Life of Love,' we can reach far beyond our own capacity and love our fellow human beings with deep compassion, because we know that all come from and are loved by God."[12] Love is attractive and what the world desperately needs today.

God formed me in life's critical moments which, through a process of re-membering, helped me to grow in wisdom and understanding, deepen my faith, and live a life of wholeness and purpose. Whether in the wilderness, valley, or mountaintop, God always opened the windows of heaven and poured out blessings—too many to count. I lost my career, but I gained my calling. Yes, it was worth it. May all of it be to the glory of God! Looking back, I see a trail of God's goodness!

STONE OF REMEMBRANCE: RECONCILIATION

In hindsight, both Callender and I returned to places where we were wounded. Callender returned after forty years, and I returned after twenty years. I don't think either one of us thought we would return under these

---

11. Hagberg and Guelich, *Critical Journey*, 154.
12. Hagberg and Guelich, *Critical Journey*, 154.

circumstances. Nor did we plan or anticipate these critical moments of personal and collective benefits. God reconciles us to himself and calls us to a ministry of reconciliation (2 Cor 5:17–19).

REFLECTION QUESTIONS

Identify a God moment in your life or ministry where God met an unknown need in an unexpected way. Why was this critical moment important to you? Who benefited from it? What long-term effect did it have on you? What is your stone of remembrance?

APPENDIX 1

We Will Not Forget!

A Prayer

> Let all that I am praise the Lord; with my whole heart, I will praise his holy name.
> Let all that I am praise the Lord; may I never forget the good things he does for me.
> (Ps 103:1–2 NLT)

Lord God,
you are amazing, compassionate, and merciful.
How great is your love!
Forgive us for those critical moments when we forget you
and turn our attention to
something else. Forgive us for not praising your holy name and always
acknowledging all your benefits.
We will not forget.

Without you, we are nothing. With you, we can be and do all things, everything you've ordained for us. With you, we can scale a wall.
There is no one like you. We are sanctified, filled with the Spirit,
empowered, gifted, and ready to follow you all the days of our lives.
We will not forget.

Appendix 1

You have enlarged our footsteps so that our feet will not slip.
We will tell the next generation about what you have done for us.
We will stand in your presence and on the rooftops
to shout about the goodness of the Lord!
We will not forget.

May many hearts be drawn to receive Jesus Christ as Lord
and Savior through our witness.
We will not forget to give you all the glory that belongs to you.
In the name of the Father, Son, and Holy Spirit. Amen.

APPENDIX 2

Stones of Remembrance at a Glance

1. *Hope*: "Be joyful in hope, patient in affliction, faithful in prayer" (Rom 12:12).

   God had brought my parents and ancestors through troubling times in America during Jim Crow and slavery. I am shaped by their hope for tomorrow. I will remember seeing my father praying and my mother singing as she washed the dishes.

   Reflection Questions: What images do you have of your parents or the people who raised you that have influenced your knowledge and relationship with God or spiritual practices? When do you recall these images? What impact do they have on you? What is your stone of remembrance?

2. *Redemption*: "Get rid of all bitterness, rage and anger, brawling and slander, along with every form of malice" (Eph 4:31).

   When I revisited Gregory's death in that police department office, God kept me from carrying hatred or bitterness toward police officers. I couldn't let this tragedy define me. God shifted my focus and gave me a different perspective to benefit my community by supporting public servants. God makes forgiveness possible. God can redeem all things for his glory.

   Reflection Questions: In reflecting on your own early childhood memories, what would your story be about? How did a profound impact help shape your beliefs or passions? Did you experience gain or loss? If so, what was it? How did it affect you? What is your stone of remembrance?

3. *Salvation*: "For God so loved the world, that he gave his only Son, that whoever believes in him should not perish but have eternal life" (John 3:16).

   I'll never forget the freedom I experienced the day Jesus set me free! Remembering my own conversion experience has allowed me to be available to the Holy Spirit as God draws others who are looking for meaning in life to himself.

   Reflection Questions: At what point in life did you receive Jesus Christ as your Lord and Savior? What effect did it have on you and others at the time? Think about a time when you shared your story with someone else. What were the circumstances and how were you impacted? What is your stone of remembrance?

4. *Peace*: "And the peace of God, which transcends all understanding, will guard your hearts and your minds in Christ Jesus" (Phil 4:7).

   Remembering what God had told me the morning I lost my job gave me peace because God revealed his will for me. Sometimes, God will prepare us for something that would normally rock our world if we had not been prepared.

   Reflection Questions: Recall a time when you received a word or message from God when the stakes were high. How did it help you understand and receive God's hand at work in your spiritual formation? What did you learn about God? What is your stone of remembrance?

5. *Sanctification*: "Therefore, since we have these promises, dear friends, let us purify ourselves from everything that contaminates body and spirit, perfecting holiness out of reverence for God" (2 Cor 7:1).

   In Greek, sanctification means "to make holy." God sanctifies us. Our role is to purify ourselves from everything that contaminates body and spirit, perfecting holiness out of reverence for God. I was learning to live in obedience to God through his word and the Spirit's leading. I was being set apart for God's will.

Stones of Remembrance at a Glance

Reflection Questions: Thinking back, can you name a specific incident in your life when it required an act of faith in life or your calling? What did you learn that kept you on course? Was there someone or something meaningful that helped along the way? In what ways did God come through in an unexpected way? What is your stone of remembrance?

6. *Guidance*: "Trust in the LORD with all your heart and lean not on your own understanding; in all your ways submit to him, and he will make your paths straight" (Prov 3:5–6).

During a long wait for my next assignment after being unemployed for a time, I was encouraged when I remembered God's word that he would enlarge my footsteps so my feet would not slip. He guided my steps in his word, through individuals and the Spirit, as I waited on him. God makes our paths straight, even when it doesn't seem like it.

Reflections Questions: Are there any God encounters when you had to wait a long time to move forward in ministry or life? If so, describe what God was working in your life as you waited. What gave you peace or unrest? What is your stone of remembrance?

7. *Faithfulness*: "He who calls you is faithful; he will surely do it" (1 Thess 5:24).

As I prepared for the second time to go to seminary, I was reminded of all the ways God had used me as I waited for the peach cobbler—how he taught me and transformed me through this waiting period. Waiting has a divine purpose.

Reflection Questions: Look back over your life to see times when you had to wait for what you thought you were ready for, but God let you know he had something else in mind. What is your peach cobbler? What did you learn after receiving it? In what ways do you celebrate now that you've received what you had been waiting for? Alone or with others? What is your stone of remembrance?

8. *Grace*: "And God is able to bless you abundantly, so that in all things at all times, having all that you need, you will abound in every good work" (2 Cor 9:8).

Appendix 2

I took it to heart when God told me to be silent and not defend myself concerning the Walker Hall matter. It was God's grace that kept me strong and hopeful that this, too, would pass. God fights our battles. He taught me a common practice to not defend myself, particularly in sensitive situations. God's grace sustains us.

Reflection Questions: Thinking back, was there a time when God gave you enough grace to trust him without your intervention or help in fixing a situation? How did you respond? What lifelong lessons did you learn and remember? What is your stone of remembrance?

9. *Calling*: "Then I heard the voice of the Lord saying, 'Whom shall I send? And who will go for us?' And I said, 'Here am I. Send me!'" (Isa 6:8).

God opened and closed doors. He taught me to listen and know his voice in whatever way he chooses to speak, and be mindful of distractions. God gave me a strong sense of calling, mobilizing me to follow the Spirit anywhere. God's calling is personal and collective; the body of Christ affirms us.

Reflection Questions: What are the circumstances and context of your calling? What did God do or say to you that kept you faithful in responding to his call, especially in a sensitive situation? What effect did it have on you and others? What did you learn or adopt as a practice? What is your stone of remembrance?

10. *Love*: "See what great love the Father has lavished on us, that we should be called children of God! And that is what we are!" (1 John 3:1).

Remembering that God so often used others to accomplish his purposes for my life has carried me through many challenging times and kept me focused on the mission. I have never felt or thought I wasn't loved by God and those he places in my life to support me. God is love. God's love radiates from us to others.

Reflection Questions: What is your story of who helped nurture, affirm, and support you for God's assignment? What effect does remembering your critical moment have on you? What was God's role? What did you learn about him? In what ways have you shared your God story with others? What is your stone of remembrance?

Stones of Remembrance at a Glance

11. *Diversity*: "For we were all baptized by one Spirit so as to form one body—whether Jews or Gentiles, slave or free—and we were all given the one Spirit to drink. Even so the body is not made up of one part but of many" (1 Cor 12:13-14).

    A glimpse of God's heavenly vision is embedded in my memory. Through the Spirit's work, it keeps me at the cross, where it is level for all peoples. God's love for diversity influences how I treat and minister to others.

    Reflection Questions: What characteristic or gift has God given you and has it become an integral part of who you are and how you engage with others? When did you first notice it and how? How are others affected by it? What is your stone of remembrance?

12. *Reconciliation*: "Therefore, if anyone is in Christ, the new creation has come: The old has gone, the new is here! All this is from God, who reconciled us to himself through Christ and gave us the ministry of reconciliation: that God was reconciling the world to himself in Christ, not counting people's sins against them. And he has committed to us the message of reconciliation" (2 Cor 5:18-19).

    In hindsight, both Callender and I returned to places where we were wounded. Callender returned after forty years, and I returned after twenty years. I don't think either one of us thought we would return under these circumstances. Nor did we plan or anticipate these critical moments of personal and collective benefits. God worked out his will.

    Reflection questions: Identify a God moment in your life or ministry whereas God met an unknown need in an unexpected way. Why was this critical moment important to you? Who benefited from it? What long-term effect did it have on you? What is your stone of remembrance?

APPENDIX 3

A Model for Remembering God's Goodness

> I will remember the deeds of the Lord; yes, I will remember your miracles of long ago. I will consider all your works and meditate on all your mighty deeds. (Ps 77:11–12)

MY APPROACH TO DEVELOPING this model is from my perspective of God encounters leading to spiritual formation, the story of Moses' calling as told in Exod 3, and the role of the body of Christ. Remembering is based on our knowledge of God's presence, plan, and work in the world, and he has included us in his story. Having a model for remembering his works is our way of honoring God's command to remember and tell others.

1. **PAY ATTENTION:** Lean into your experience. In what ways is God trying to get your attention? Identify the Holy Spirit's work. See, listen, pray, discern, and journal regularly.

2. **BRING INTO FOCUS:** Assess how the spiritual encounter aligns or fits a concern or area God has already placed in your heart as a burden, passion, or interest. Who has God brought into your life recently, and for what purposes? Who is praying for you? Where do you see the fingerprints of God? Doors are opening and closing for a reason.

3. **SATISFY YOUR SPIRITUAL CURIOSITY:** Lean in further by recognizing that God is trying to tell you something. What Scriptures, biblical stories, or images come to mind when you think about what you are hearing from God? Ask a spiritual companion to assist in the discernment process. God knows what is on your mind and in your

A Model for Remembering God's Goodness

heart. Have you had one or more affirmations: others' stories, dreams, Scriptures, burdens, visions, or it comes up in various conversations? Take time to test your call and God's plan for spiritual formation using a framework such as *The Critical Journey*.

4. **RECOGNIZE ANY RESISTANCE:** What are your concerns? What's holding you back? Name any negative influences or previous setbacks. Be aware of feelings or thoughts of not being equipped or in your comfort zone. Who is modeling who God has called you to be and do? Only some people will recognize, support, and understand your calling. Are there any institutional, theological, or social and cultural barriers? Unveil any hidden agendas of others. Pray for those who oppose you.

5. **BEHOLD GOD'S CALLING:** Be in his presence, for the ground you stand on is holy. Be vulnerable before God. Watch, listen, and pray. Where are you experiencing peace? What images are propelling you to take the next step?

6. **GIVE A RADICAL RESPONSE TO GOD:** You are available and willing to follow Jesus wherever he leads you. Your name is on the assignment. Express your openness to his expectations for using your God-given gifts, presence, voice, and influence in oral or written communications. "And I said, 'Here am I. Send me!'" (Isa 6:8). "Be strong and courageous. Do not be afraid; do not be discouraged, for the Lord your God will be with you wherever you go" (Josh 1:9).

7. **CELEBRATE WHAT GOD IS DOING:** This is God's story and should be celebrated. Practice the presence of God based on Brother Lawrence's book *Practicing the Presence of God*. Be in fellowship with the Creator no matter what you are involved in, noise or quiet. Make celebrations personal and community-focused, as well as a daily practice and way of life. Celebrate God advancing his kingdom through your calling and service.

APPENDIX 4

The Stages in the Life of Faith

The Critical Journey

LATER IN LIFE, ONE of the books most helpful to me in understanding spiritual formation was *The Critical Journey*, written by Janet O. Hagberg and Robert A. Guelich. The authors note, "The journey is the place of mystery, holy ground. . . . It involves bringing our response in sync with God's grace in our lives."[1] Without God's grace, we cannot move through spiritual formation on our own. Sometimes, movement will require the help of someone else, like "a faith community, friends, a support group, family, pastor or priest, spiritual director, counselor, or even a therapist."[2]

I highlighted the six stages of spiritual formation in the faith journey as follows:[3]

STAGE ONE: "The Recognition of God"—the acknowledgment that God is present in heaven and on earth. There is a sense of need and/or awe of God.

STAGE TWO: "The Life of Discipleship"—the life of nurture, learning, and belonging with companions to help guide the way as role models.

---

1. Hagberg and Guelich, *Critical Journey*, 14.
2. Hagberg and Guelich, *Critical Journey*, 14.
3. These descriptions are based on the stages outlined in Hagberg and Guelich, *Critical Journey*.

The Stages in the Life of Faith

STAGE THREE: "The Productive Life"—the opportunity to serve others based on your spiritual gifts and skills.

STAGE FOUR: "The Journey Inward"—the need for introspection by going deep into one's inner journey because of something unsettling in your life. The individual is looking to God for answers.

THE WALL: the difficult time in an individual's life guided by God and requiring total dependence on him to see them through. One is drawn to surrender.

STAGE FIVE: "The Journey Outward"—its focus is outward from a new perspective of being in God's will instead of our own.

STAGE SIX: "The Life of Love"—the reflection of God is seen by others through our life in practice and service. We die to ourselves. Obedience to God becomes a natural part of life.

Bibliography

Antonaccio, Egidio. *Dream Cottage*. 1993. Oil, 20 × 30," Olivetti Corporation, Ivrea, Italy. Print distributed courtesy of Art Licensing Partners, Walnut Creek, CA.

Berkholz, Margrit. "Synopsis of Talk by Sara Synder, Grateful Home." In *Shelter, Women and Development*, edited by Hemalata Dandekar, 148–49. Ann Arbor: Wahr, 1993.

Chambers, Oswald. *My Utmost for His Highest*. Westwood, NJ: Bardour, 1963.

Christian Reformed Church. "Heidelberg Catechism." In *Ecumenical Creeds and Reformed Confessions*. Grand Rapids: Christian Reformed Church, 1988.

———. "Women in Ecclesiastical Office." https://www.crcna.org/welcome/beliefs/position-statements/women-ecclesiastical-office.

Cubitt, Geoffrey. *History and Memory*. New York: Manchester University Press, 2007.

Dawson, Shay. "Ruby Bridges." Edited by Corina Gonzalez. National Women's History Museum, June 20, 2025. https://www.womenshistory.org/education-resources/biographies/ruby-bridges.

DeHaan, Dan. *The God You Can Know*. Chicago: Moody, 1982.

Elliott, Meagan, et al. *History's Future in the North End*. Urban and Regional Planning Program, Taubman College of Architecture and Urban Planning, University of Michigan, May 2013. https://taubmancollege.umich.edu/student-work/historys-future-in-the-north-end/.

Friedman, Edwin H. *A Failure of Nerve: Leadership in the Age of the Quick Fix*. New York: Church, 2007.

Hagberg, Janet O., and Robert A. Guelich. *The Critical Journey: Stages in the Life of Faith*. Dallas: Word, 1989.

Horton, Harold. *The Gifts of the Spirit*. Springfield, MO: Gospel House, 1975.

Meehan, Chris. "A Blessing in Disguise." *Kalamazoo Gazette*, Apr. 21, 2001.

Miranda, Lin-Manuel. "It's Quiet Uptown." Performed by Renée Elise Goldsberry and Lin-Manuel Miranda. Track 18, act 2 in *Hamilton (Original Broadway Cast Recording)*. New York: Atlantic, 2015.

Mulholland, M. Robert, Jr. *Invitation to a Journey: A Road Map for Spiritual Formation*. Downers Grove, IL: InterVarsity, 2016.

National Archives. "Brown v. Board of Education (1954)." Milestone Documents, last updated Mar. 18, 2024. https://www.archives.gov/milestone-documents/brown-v-board-of-education.

———. "The Great Migration (1910–1970)." African American Heritage, last updated June 28, 2021. https://www.archives.gov/research/african-americans/migrations/great-migration.

Bibliography

Nouwen, Henri J. M. *Discernment: Reading the Signs of Daily Life.* New York: HarperOne, 2015.

———. *The Wounded Healer.* New York: Doubleday, 1979.

Odom, David L. "The Seven Year Itch." Faith and Leadership, Faith and Education at Duke Divinity. https://faithandleadership.com/the-seven-year-itch.

Palmer, Parker. "The Broken-Open Heart." *Weavings* 24.2 (2009) 1–12. Repr., Nashville: Upper Room, 2008. https://couragerenewal.org/wp-content/uploads/2022/06/PJP-WeavingsArticle-Broken-OpenHeart.pdf.

Parker, Jennifer. "CRC's First Black Pastor Returns 42 Years After Bitter Farewell." *Banner,* May 21, 2001. https://network.crcna.org/sites/default/files/Callendar.pdf.

Person, Dave. "Diversity in the Pulpit." *Kalamazoo Gazette,* Nov. 13, 1999.

Posie, Denise L. "Rising with New Courage and New Hope." *Weavings* 24.2 (2009). Repr., Nashville: Upper Room, 2008.

Rausch, Thomas P. *An 8 Day Ignatian Retreat for Priests, Religious, Deacons, and Lay Ministers.* Mahwah, NJ: Paulist, 2008.

Schuman, Josie. "Black Forgiveness Is Not for White People." *Carroll News* (Huntsville, VA), Oct. 21, 2020. https://carrollnews.org/4367/opinion/black-forgiveness-is-not-for-white-people/.

Speed, Billy Cheney. "Dan DeHaan Put His Heart into His Faith." *Atlanta Constitutional,* Feb. 27, 1982. https://www.newspapers.com/article/the-atlanta-constitution-dan-dehaan-put/46764682/.

Van Sant, Gus, dir. *Finding Forrester.* Produced by Columbia Pictures. Culver City, CA: Sony Pictures Releasing, 2000. 2 hours, 16 minutes. https://play.google.com/store/movies/details/Finding_Forrester?gl=US&hl=en&id=ucrkYFdFty8.

The Village Idiom. "Take a Licking and Keep On Kicking." https://www.thevillageidiom.org/idioms/take-a-licking-and-keep-on-ticking-idiom-meaning-and-origin/.

Whyte, David. "The Journey." https://allpoetry.com/poem/15379826-The-Journey-by-David-Whyte.

www.ingramcontent.com/pod-product-compliance
Lightning Source LLC
Chambersburg PA
CBHW071725090426
42738CB00009B/1881